Insights of a
Himalayan Pilgrim

Insights
of a Himalayan
Pilgrim

Lama Anagarika Govinda

DHARMA  PUBLISHING

Tibetan Art and Culture Series

Sacred Art of Tibet
Psycho-cosmic Symbolism of the Buddhist Stupa
Insights of a Himalayan Pilgrim
Tibet in Pictures
Art of Enlightenment
Gesar! The Wondrous Adventures of Gesar, King of Ling

Library of Congress Cataloging-in-Publication Data

Govinda, Anagarika Brahmacari.
  Insights of a Himalayan pilgrim.

  (Tibetan art and culture series)
  1.Buddhism—China—Tibet. 2. Buddhism—
Doctrines. I. Title. II. Series.

BQ7612.G68 1990   294.3'923   90-3719
ISBN 0-89800-213-3   ISBN 0-89800-204-4 (pbk.)

Frontispiece courtesy of Gesar Magazine
Photographs on pp. 2, 58, 83, 88 by Li Gotami Govinda

Typeset in Merganthaler Palatino and printed in the USA
by Dharma Press, Oakland, California

01 00 99 98 97 96 95 94 93 92 91   10 9 8 7 6 5 4 3 2 1

To all pilgrims on the spiritual path

Contents

Illustrations

Introduction

Lama Govinda (1898–1985) has earned a prominent place in the history of Buddhism in the West. His early interest in Buddhism led him from his native Germany to Burma and Sri Lanka, where he studied and practiced within the Theravadin tradition and built a country hermitage as his permanent residence. While attending a conference in Darjeeling, in northern India, his life took an unexpected turn. During his visit to the surrounding mountains, he found himself caught in a Himalayan blizzard and took refuge in a Tibetan monastery. There he met his guru, Tomo Geshe, and began a new phase of his pilgrimage.

The Himalayas became his home for the next fifty years. The lamas and monasteries of that mountainous region nurtured his education in Tibetan Buddhist teachings and practices. He became an Indian national, and founded a small ashram in the Kumaon Himalaya for study and meditation. He traveled extensively in Central and Western Tibet and in 1948 followed the ancient pilgrim's path that cir-cumambulates Mount Kailas. In the cave temples of Tsaparang, Western Tibet, he discovered a wealth of tenth-century art, which he and his wife Li Gotami made great efforts to record. Their paintings of Tibet have been on exhibit in many of India's major cities, and Li Gotami's photographs of the artistic treasures of Central and Western Tibet were published in *Tibet in Pictures* (Dharma Publishing 1979).

Introducing *Tibet in Pictures*, Lama Govinda points out the depth of knowledge developed within the Tibetan Buddhist tradition and its great value to the Western world:

'And here we come to the problem of our time: we have learned to master the forces of nature, but we have not yet achieved mastery over ourselves, our inner life, our psychic and spiritual forces, in short, the dormant faculties of our deeper consciousness, which after all created the world in which we live and all that we have achieved in the form of manifold civilizations. These faculties permit us to see the fundamental one-ness of life, the interrelatedness of all peoples and civilizations and the ultimate oneness of humanity; they even allow us our conquest over the forces of nature. Yet we do not understand these faculties.

'. . . Tibet chose to cultivate and develop [these] powers of inner perception, which are the very source of all human culture, knowledge, and achievement.

Unless man is able to coordinate, unify, and ultimately integrate these powers within himself and thereby become complete, how can he expect to create a harmonious and united human world? This is the way Tibetans viewed the problem of the future of humanity, a problem that now faces us on a global scale.'

After 1959, at a time when Tibetan Buddhism was nearly unknown in the West and invasions were endangering its very survival, Lama Govinda increased his efforts to communicate the great value of this tradition to the West. His first book, *Foundations of Tibetan Mysticism*, was widely read by students of religion and Buddhism, creating a receptive audience for the works that followed: *The Psychological Attitude of Early Buddhist Philosophy, The Way of the White Clouds, Creative Meditation and Multi-Dimensional Consciousness*, and *Psycho-cosmic Symbolism of the Buddhist Stupa*.

Lama Govinda's lectures in America and Europe did much to demystify Tibetan Buddhism and introduce its practical teachings on mind and mental development. Through his presence, his compassion, and his inner strength, he exemplified the transforming power of these teachings to thousands of people, including those assembled at the Vatican, where he spoke at the Pope's request. He spent the last years of his life in Mill Valley, California, a short distance north of San Francisco. During the 1970's he gave several talks at the Nyingma Institute in Berkeley; he also wrote articles for *Crystal Mirror* and *Gesar Magazine*, and worked with Dharma Publishing editors to prepare *Tibet in Pictures* for publication.

Insights of a Himalayan Pilgrim is a gesture of appreciation for Lama Govinda and his pioneering efforts to communicate the value of Tibetan Buddhism to the West. It brings together essays that have appeared in *Crystal Mirror, Gesar,* and *The Middle Way* with other articles that were recently translated from German by the Dharma Publishing staff. We are grateful to Ven. Advayavajra, President of the Lama and Li Gotami Govinda Foundation, for permission to publish the materials in this book and for his careful review of the manuscript.

An eloquent spokesman for the inner pilgrimage that evokes the 'essential miracle' of realization, Lama Govinda defines the true pilgrim as one who follows his or her inner promptings towards truth. While the path may be slightly different for each individual, following this path involves total surrender to the process of inner exploration. In his compassionate embodiment of this path, Lama Govinda exemplified the 'Himalayan Pilgrim.' His devotion and courage shine through this collection of essays, an inspiration to all who undertake the pilgrim's path.

Editor's Note

Well-versed in Pali, Sanskrit, and Tibetan, Lama Govinda drew readily upon all three languages when expressing significant Buddhist terms. For the ease of the general reader, the terms in this book are given in Sanskrit wherever possible and spelled the way Western readers are most accustomed to seeing them. Diacriticals are not used; "c" becomes "ch" and "ṣ" and "ś" are both spelled "sh." For example, the Sanskrit name Śākyamuni becomes Shakyamuni, and the term Prajñāpāramitā becomes Prajnaparamita. Where it is clear that Lama Govinda preferred the Pali or Tibetan term, or when the context best suits that term, we have retained it. Please consult "Significant Terms" on pp. 182–85 for Pali equivalents and standard transcriptions of Sanskrit terms. For further study, The chart of "Basic Categories" on pp. 186–87 provides Sanskrit, Tibetan, and English of some traditional categories of terms referred to in the text.

Part One

THE PATH OF TRUTH

Pilgrims and Monasteries in the Himalayas

To see the greatness of a mountain, one must keep one's distance; to understand its form, one must move around it; to experience its moods, one must see it at sunrise and sunset, at noon and at midnight, in sun and in rain, in snow and in storm, in summer and in winter and in all the other seasons. He who can see the mountain like this comes near to the life of the mountain, a life that is as intense and varied as that of a human being.

The Way of the White Clouds

The Himalayas are not only the highest and mightiest mountains in the world—awe-inspiring by their mere vastness—they are also the meeting place of the most ancient and spiritually advanced civilizations of the world. Like a gigantic magnet, the Himalayas seemed to attract the best that each passing age and culture had to offer. Blending the wisdom and art of many nations and ages, they retained them in the shelters of protected valleys and in the fastnesses of the highlands.

Though the mountains acted as a barrier to physical forces and the worldly ambitions of kings and conquerors, they were no obstacle to the exchange of spiritual achievements and to the cultivation and preservation of ancient traditions. On the contrary, they acted as a restraining, selective, and purifying factor, separating the chaff from the grain, the base metal from the gold, and the trivial and superficial from the genuine. The mountains are therefore a challenge to the human spirit. Only those who have the strength and endurance to stand up to such a challenge can survive in this world.

The challenge of the mountains is twofold. On the one hand, nature presents itself in such enchanting beauty and grandeur that creations of human origin appear to be dwarfed and insignificant in comparison. On the other hand, nature displays its ferocious and destructive forces which challenge the very existence of man.

But the more a man has to struggle against the adverse forces of nature, the greater is the intensity of his inner life and of his creative imagination. In order to balance the powerful influences of the external world, he has to build up his own inner world. This, however, does not happen in an entirely independent or arbitrary way, but according to certain laws. The deeper a man looked within himself, the more it dawned upon him that these laws were the same which created the rhythm of mountains, the eternal

4

song of streams and waterfalls, the fury of blizzards, and the silent beauty of snow and clouds. And it was this discovery which gave man the strength to accept the twofold challenge of nature and made the Himalayas the abode of saints and sages, as well as the refuge of those who were seekers of truth and beauty, of bodily and spiritual health.

The profound parallelism of body and soul, spiritual and natural laws, inner and outer forces, is nowhere more capable of direct experiment than in the mountains, and of all mountains nowhere more than in the Himalayas where thousands of years of human devotion have created an atmosphere and tradition which is unequalled by any other region in the world. It is an atmosphere of devotion, which is older than any organized religion or dogma, though many a religious belief may have grown out of it and many systems of religious interpretation may have been superimposed on it.

"In the oldest religion, everything was alive, not supernaturally but naturally alive . . . For the whole life-effort of man was to get his life into contact with the elemental life of the cosmos, mountain-life, cloud-life, thunder-life, air-life, earth-life, sun-life. To come into immediate *felt* contact, and so to derive energy, power, and a dark sort of joy. This effort into sheer naked contact, *without an intermediary or mediator,* is the root meaning of religion."   —D. H. Lawrence

5

Such a religion is truly universal, and if there is something that is characteristic of the mental outlook of the Himalayan people, it is this ancient and universal religion which flows like a mighty stream through all the various faiths and traditions. And it is this immediate contact with the elemental life of the cosmos (which in our intellectual conceit and shortsightedness we try to dismiss as "primitive animism") which thousands of pilgrims seek year after year in the sacred mountains of the Himalayas under the guise of religious creeds and symbols.

Of all Himalayan pilgrimages, that of Mount Kailas[1] (which itself is situated in the Trans-Himalayan Range) is regarded to be the greatest and holiest by Hindus and Buddhists alike, and may therefore serve as a typical example. Whether Kailas is spoken of as the "throne of the gods" and the "Abode of Shiva and Parvati," or as the "Mandala of Dhyani-Buddhas and Bodhisattvas," or as "Meru," the spiritual and phenomenal center of our world, the fact which is expressed in the symbolic language of different traditions is the experience of a higher reality which is conveyed through a strange combination of natural and spiritual phenomena, which even those who are unaffected by religious beliefs cannot escape.

Like a gigantic temple, rising in regular tiers of horizontal ledges and in perfect symmetry, Kailas marks the center of the "Roof of the World," the heart of the biggest temple, the seat and center of cosmic powers, the axis which connects the earth with the universe, the super-antenna for the influx and outflow of the spiritual energies of our planet.

The great rhythm of nature pervades everything, and man is woven into it. His imagination is no more a matter of individual fancy; it becomes an instrument of those forces which govern the movements of suns and planets, of oceans and continents, winds and clouds. Imagination here becomes an adequate expression of reality on the plane of human consciousness. Here the gods that were buried in the subconscious regions of the human mind for thousands of years, until their memory had become mere shadows and phantoms, appear again before the pilgrim. Hearing their voices and seeing their radiance, the pilgrim knows that he can never lose them again in all his life, because he has been face to face with the Eternal.

Thus, the pilgrim feels himself surrounded by many subtle influences, which in accordance with various religious traditions have been described as the presence of divine powers. Whatever their origin or their definition, there is no doubt that a strange transformation of consciousness takes place in those elevated regions and especially around those time-honored places of pilgrimage. One becomes sensitive and open to new realities; in short, the intuitive faculties of the mind are awakened and stimulated.

Thus, many of those who felt the call to a life of religious devotion and meditation took advantage of these ideal conditions: some as hermits in solitary caves and hermitages, others in small groups or in monastic communities. The development of the latter was particularly favored by the highly organized character of Tibetan Buddhism, which exerts its influence over the greater part of the Himalayas and far beyond the confines of Tibet proper: from Ladakh in the west to Bhutan in the east.

While Hindu sanctuaries and those of local deities are generally confined to isolated temples and wayside shrines, according to the more individualistic and therefore the less organized character of Hinduism, Buddhist monasteries, wherever they are found, have grown into a dominating feature of Himalayan life and landscape. They do not dominate as something that has been forced upon their surroundings, but rather as something that has grown out of them.

There is a deep inner relationship between those mountains and monasteries. They are the true embodiment of the spirit of the Himalayas. What mountains and monasteries have in common is greatness, simplicity, strength, and aloofness. The sloping lines of mighty mountains are repeated in the slanting walls of massive architecture.

The inner relationship of man and nature is nowhere more strongly expressed than in those mighty citadels of faith, the monasteries of the Himalayas:

8

"Proudly isolated on summits beaten by the wind, amidst wild landscapes, Tibetan Gompas (monasteries) look vaguely aggressive, as if bidding defiance to invisible foes, at the four corners of the horizon. Or, when squatting between high mountain ranges, they often assume a disquieting air of laboratories where occult forces are manipulated. That twofold appearance corresponds to a certain reality. The hard conquest of a world other than that perceived through the senses, transcendental knowledge, mystic realizations, mastery over occult forces, such were the aims for the pursuit of which were built the lamaist towering citadels and those enigmatic cities concealed in the maze of snowy hills."

Alexandra David-Neel

Whenever beauty, solitude, and grandeur produce an atmosphere of awe and religious inspiration, there will be found a sanctuary, a hermitage, or a monastery. Many of them were founded by monks and mystics who retired into caves in order to meditate in the stillness and purity of nature. Such caves were later enlarged, decorated with wall paintings, and turned into temples, around which new dwellings were constructed or carved into the living rock until a complete monastery came into existence.

In other places, the disciples of a hermit built their huts around that of their Guru, either on the lofty summit of a solitary mountain or on top of an isolated rock-formation, out of which in the course of time grew bigger and statelier buildings. Where the conditions were favorable, temples and libraries, assembly-halls, courtyards, storehouses, and dwelling quarters for students and guests were added; and finally, complete monastic cities came into existence, in which hundreds and, in some cases, even thousands of monks were living.

A third type of monastery is that which has been carved into the face of sheer cliffs. All their temples, living quarters, corridors, staircases, etc., are carved into the living rock, and only verandahs and windows, sometimes adorned with decorative carvings, are visible from the outside. Some of these rock-monasteries have elaborate facades with balconies, projecting roofs, and other architectural additions which make the whole structure look like a swallow's nest hanging on to the rock high above the valley.

These monasteries are the chief sources of culture, the strongholds of civilization in the untamed wilderness of the inner Himalayas and far into the Trans-Himalayan regions. They are the fortresses of man against the hostile forces of nature. And yet, as already pointed out, they are the fulfillment of nature on a higher plane, as they express its spirit more than any other thing. This proves their greatness as works of architecture.

In spite of the primitiveness of the materials used, Tibeto-Himalayan architecture is most effective and often of monumental dimensions, like the palace of the former kings of western Tibet at Leh, or some of the bigger monasteries in Ladakh, Spiti, Lahaul, and other Himalayan countries. In the southeastern Himalayas, similar architectural forms are combined with slanting and peaked wooden roofs suitable for the more humid climate.

What, however, is common to all of them is their emphasis on solidity, strength, massiveness, and monumental greatness. They try to emphasize the substantiality and weightiness of matter. This purpose is achieved aesthetically, not only by the use of slanting lines of walls and windows, but also by accentuating the edges of their flat roofs with dark red-brown cornices which form a heavy horizontal line (like the protruding edge of a lid), separating most effectively the white or light-ocher walls from the dark blue of the sky. When buildings rise up in a terrace-like fashion, as is usually the case with big monasteries, these red-brown cornices are like the punctuation in a rising rhythm, beautifully setting off one building against the other. The same device is used for the small roof-like cornices over every window and verandah and over the main entrances of monastic buildings, for which this decoration is exclusively reserved.

It certainly can be said that this architecture has created a maximum of effect with a minimum of build-

11

ing material and technical aid. It has created something so powerful and noble that it appeals to people of all races and times. It is, truly speaking, a timeless architecture, which the pilgrim of the Himalayas will always associate with the eternal peaks and the profound peace of these far-off regions. He will cherish the memory of those mysteriously challenging citadels of faith in which the aspirations of the human soul have found such perfect expression, and he will keep their challenge in his heart like a talisman, until, perhaps, one day he will find himself on the way towards the realization of his ultimate aim.

Notes

1. *See* Lama Anagarika Govinda, *The Way of the White Clouds* (Berkeley: Shambhala, 1970), p. 198ff.

Hinduism
and Buddhism

Nowadays many people believe that Buddhism is a kind of reform movement within Hinduism and lump both religions together. But in reality it is different: Each of the two religions developed from completely different roots of Indian spirituality.

If we look today at the mighty stream of the Indian tradition as a whole, which flows from the darkness of prehistoric times to the present, then we recognize that Buddhism—as well as Jainism—came from a source welling beneath the surface for more than a millenium of Indo-Aryan supremacy. In the sixth century B.C. it rose into full view and claimed its rightful place *next to* Indo-Aryan Brahmanism: not in complete opposition to Brahmanism, but unmistakably different and distinct. If we want to understand what the Buddha taught, we have to be clearly aware of these differences.

But first we have to keep in mind that in the sixth century B.C. there was nothing which could be called

"Hinduism"—even the term "Hinduism" was not coined before the twelfth century when the Muslim conquerors called those people who were living beyond the Sindhu river "Hindus," and created with the term "Hinduism" a general description of their faith.

At no time was there in India just *one* religion. Just as there exist hundreds of languages and dialects, there are hundreds of religious groups. "Hinduism" as we know it today is a generic term for the different religions of India which developed in the course of the centuries, most of which did not yet exist at the time of the Buddha. Hinduism in its present wealth of forms is the result of a merging of Brahmanism, Buddhism, Jainism, and many other cults and sects. If we want to talk about "Hinduism," we first have to be clear which lineage we want to talk about: Shivaism, Shaktism, or Vaishnavism in its many different forms, or Shankaracarya's *advaita* philosophy, to name just a few of the most well-known lineages.

Besides these forms of Indian religions, there are in present-day India Muslims, Parsis, Christians, and even Jews, who formed their first communities in the first century A.D. in Malabar. (When these Jews tried to return to Israel a few decades ago, they soon came back deeply disappointed, because they experienced the people there as completely foreign. The old tradition of the Indian Jews made them feel so different from the present generation of Jews being raised in the

West that they could not find a way to fit into such a society. This exemplifies that India has a specific way of dealing with human beings who are very different from each other based on a great tolerance for diverse religious beliefs.)

While in this century many people in Europe and many Western scientists were of the opinion that Buddhism was a reform movement within Brahmanism, in the nineteenth century many scholars held that there was a relationship between Brahmanism and Buddhism similar to that between Christianity and Judaism. They took it for granted that at the time of the Buddha the majority of the people in India were adherents of the Vedic religion, and therefore considered it evident that the Buddha took his teachings and ideas from the Brahmanic religion.

Even today this opinion is expressed by learned philosphers. Dr. Radhakrishnan, former president of India and professor of philosophy, held, along with his students, that Buddhism was nothing but a specific variation of Hinduism. But this is a very unscientific perspective; today we know much more about this historic period and can see that, besides Brahmanism, there existed many other religions which were not officially recognized, since the invading Aryans, who came from the north, had suppressed the original, highly developed culture, perhaps an even higher culture than that of the conquerers.

Since history shows that the conquerers of a people with higher culture lose their identity relatively soon, the Indo-Aryans tried to protect themselves through a social system which excluded everybody who did not belong to their society and religion. As was also done in Greece, they consequently introduced a system of castes which distinguished between people, first, on the basis of their color *(varna)*, and second, on the basis of their profession *(jati)*. Jati actually means family, since the son had to embrace his father's profession whether he was qualified to do so or not: Whoever was born a brahmin, *was* a brahmin, and whoever was born a shudra, remained a shudra. Those who belonged neither to one nor the other caste (i.e., the original people of low social status) were considered the ones without caste, who did not deserve a real "existence."

This division was carried to such extremes that even if the shadow of a person without caste fell upon a brahmin, he would feel impure and defiled. The Hindus belonging to a caste had special signals which informed those without caste to leave the main road and to behave at the roadside in such a way that in passing by the Hindu of caste would not feel defiled by having to look at them. The present Indian government is trying to do away with the distinctions and prejudices of the castes, but this is opposed in the villages where brahmins and the ones without caste still fetch their water from different wells. It is difficult to overcome habits and "natural orders" which have been in existence for millenia.

Yet the caste system was only one pillar of the Vedic religion. The second pillar was *yajna* or sacrifice. Only those belonging to the higher castes could conduct a sacrifice; all others were excluded. Ritualistic conduct was the privilege of the brahmins. Since sacrifice was of predominant importance—as with all Aryan peoples—and the whole social structure was based upon it, the brahmin caste did of course take advantage of it. Even the kings had to bow down before brahmins when they were conducting a sacrifice. And since these sacrifices consisted for the most part of the sacrifice of living beings, the idea of *ahimsa* (nonviolence, not harming), which is so characteristic of Jainism, Buddhism, and contemporary Hinduism, was totally unknown to the Vedas: The Vedic-Brahmanic religion did not know the idea of *ahimsa*.

It was Gandhi who in the recent past once again brought the idea of *ahimsa* to the awareness of the Indian people, made it popular, and based his whole world view on it. Therefore the question naturally arises: When in the course of Indian history did this idea emerge for the first time? For these ideas do not just pop up out of nowhere; they remain in the background for a long time until the time is right.

Three Indian religious-philosophical movements, all of them more ancient than Buddhism, very early included respect for all forms of life—i.e., *ahimsa*—in their code of ethics: the movement of the shramanas, the Jains, and the Sankhya philosophers. Even today, the monks of the strictest schools of Jainism wear a protective piece of cloth in front of their mouths lest they inadvertently inhale tiny insects and thereby become guilty of killing living beings. Buddhism, which could be regarded as part of the shramana religions, never went to that extreme, but also upheld the idea of *ahimsa*.

In about 500 B.C., the idea of karma emerged in these same circles of the shramanas, Jains, and Sankhya philosophers. One can read the Vedas from cover to cover without finding any mention of the teachings of karma, which in our time appear to be so typical of the Hindu-dharma.

Therefore we have to ask ourselves, how did the ideas of *ahimsa* and karma find their way into present-day Hinduism? And this will bring us to the main point of our inquiry: Contemporary Hinduism is the product of a synthesis of Aryan Brahmanism and essential elements of the shramana religions, Buddhism, and Jainism, which took place in the first millennium A.D., mainly because of Buddhism. This is because after the time of King Ashoka (about 250 B.C.), Buddhism was for centuries the predominant religion of India. Through the great universities of north and northeast India, which were built and maintained by Buddhists, Buddhism influenced the entire culture of the subcontinent and beyond, in a kind of "cultural colonialism" that included most Asian countries.

It was with Shankaracharya (about 800 A.D.) that Hinduism proper, as we know it today, emerged as a kind of reform movement. Diverse elements of popular religious beliefs, but above all the fundamental principles of Buddhism, were incorporated, although subordinated to the basic ideas of Brahmanism. The result is modern Hinduism. Without doubt Hinduism is a remarkable and wonderful religion and—in my opinion—there is reason neither for antagonism nor for arguing against Hinduism. But we should also be clearly aware of the differences and not gloss over them. Whoever wishes to follow a particular religion has to know it very well and be clear about why he prefers it. It would be quite senseless to just accept a world view which is not understood, or which one has not gained by one's own insight.

The main difference between Hinduism and Buddhism is that Hinduism is based upon a theological principle, while Buddhism is non-theistic. In the Buddhist tradition, if we talk about various deities, we are actually talking about the various aspects of our own consciousness, which are humanized and depicted by gods and goddesses. The Buddha himself never objected in any way to the idea of the Vedic deities. He maintained the position, however, that it is of little importance what somebody believes. What is most important is to act in accord with one's belief

19

system. Thus he explained that it is all right to believe in Brahma—the Vedic creator god—but one should not become dependent on such a belief. And this was the point in his teachings about the idea of karma. As soon as one believes in karma, however, the belief in external deities becomes unimportant, because one can no longer believe in being at the mercy of gods and other external forces. One attains maturity and realizes that dependency is possible only with regard to one's own conscience—with regard to karma, that is, our own actions in thought, word, and deed.

Many people misunderstand the teaching of karma in the sense of a kind of "fate" which cannot be influenced, or as some kind of automatic mechanism. But this is exactly what the Buddha did not want to express with "karma." In his disputes with the teachings of the Jains, who understand karma as an external course of action independent of our intentions, he explained that karma is an act of volition: Where there is no volition, or intention *(cetana)*, no karma is created.

Thus, one can dream of killing somebody, but this does not mean that one is a murderer. Those images and ideas which emerge in the dream consciousness do not necessarily have to be an expression of volitional intention; a dream is not within the reach of conscious control. Since it is non-volitional, it does not create karma. Perhaps it is possible to illustrate the different ideas of karma of the Jains and Buddhists in this way: If a mason, standing on a scaffold, suddenly and unintentionally drops a brick which then hits and kills a pedestrian, the mason is not a murderer. According neither to modern laws nor to Buddhist understanding is he guilty—even despite having possibly been careless—since he did not have the intention to kill; therefore he has to be acquitted. However, according to Buddhist understanding, the same man would have been a murderer, if, with the intention of killing a certain person, he had dropped the brick—even if the brick missed that person. In other words, it is the intention which creates karma, not merely the external events. The deed, the activity (karma) is always monitored by conscious volition; it is never a random act.

Here again it becomes evident that the Buddha traced contemporary ideas (in this case the understanding of karma held by the Jains and other shramana sects of his time) back to their ancient, original understanding. Thus he said about himself, "I did not invent the Dharma: It is the Dharma of ancient times." But this statement in particular has always been neglected by modern scholars and researchers, who thought that the Buddha was referring to the past only in order to make clear that his teachings were something like a universal law; they did not take his statement seriously from the historical point of view, since they were unable to prove it.

But today we know that there once existed a unique, great pre-Aryan culture, which developed about 3000 B.C. in northwestern India. In 1922 the cities of Harappa and Mohenjo-Daro were first unearthed; since that time many other cities have been discovered, presenting a culture comparable to those of ancient Egypt, Assyria, and Sumeria. The people of that time obviously knew how to write, although nobody has yet been able to decode their written language. Not too long ago a scholar was of the opinion that the god Shiva was already known at the time of the Indus culture. This seems very likely. In this case we could also assume that the ideas of Shivaism were at that time already developed to a certain extent, but as of yet we do not have any direct evidence.

After the invasion of the Indo-Aryans this culture went underground. Possibly it was Dravidic. The Dravidians—today living in the south of India—speak languages which are completely different from those of northern India. And even though the Dravidians of southern India are today Hindus too, many of their ideas are different from those of the north. Here some concepts were preserved—although they were later written down in Sanskrit—which most likely stem from prehistoric times.

How was it possible that Buddhism and the Buddha with his Dharma could conquer India so quickly? Adhering to the idea of *ahimsa*, Buddhism was opposed to any form of violence. Its "weapon," not immediately recognizable as such, was the introduction of the idea of karma with a new and more psychological meaning. If one understands what karma really means, then it becomes immediately evident that the existence of deities or that of a creator god is superfluous, or at least unimportant, since human beings are no longer under the seeming sway of these deities. Deities turn out to be unreal, illusory, or merely a suggestion which we have allowed to have power over us. Gods may be existent or not, but whatever they are, they do not have the power to change our lives—they are themselves subject to the law of karma.

Many of these ideas can be found in the early Upanishads. Since they were composed at about the Buddha's time, between the fifth and sixth centuries B.C., they could have influenced his thinking. But if this were so, why were they secret teachings transmitted only to a few? And in that case the Buddha would very likely have never heard about them, since he belonged to the warrior caste, not to that of the brahmins. This is the reason why it seems more likely that the earliest Upanishads, and for certain the later Upanishads, were influenced by Buddhism and not the other way around. It is especially remarkable that these Upanishads, although supposedly a continuation of the Brahmanic tradition, introduced ideas and concepts which were contradictory to the principles of Brahmanism and the Vedas.

For example, they taught a spiritualization of the until then bloody sacrifices at which thousands of innocent animals were killed, although nobody thought of sacrificing himself—or his "self." (And in spite of all the reforms which followed during the next thousand years, goats and other animals are still "sacrificed" every day in India, residues of an ancient past when it was thought possible to bribe the gods with sacrifice: "I give you a cow or a horse, and you give me what I desire: victory over my enemies, or many descendants, or riches.")

With the public appearance of the shramana religions and the change in thinking of large segments of the population who increasingly followed the ideal of *ahimsa*, it became the custom, as in Buddhism, to give flowers, fruits, food, and incense as an offering. And since because of the teachings of karma the deities became "powerless," it was no longer necessary to bribe them, a change the kings and merchants especially enjoyed, because the sacrifices were very expensive for them. The teaching of karma also made it unnecessary to oppose the deities—if people wanted to worship them, they could do so: Karma was incorruptible and even the mightiest of the deities, even the creator god, was subject to its law.

The sixth century B.C. was characterized by a major religious movement in which people left the security of family relationships and renounced the life of a householder. These renunciates roamed from place to place, begged for food, and slept underneath trees. Some wore their hair long, others shaved their heads.

They did not have any other rules than not to harm other sentient beings and to meditate. They taught what they had understood in the depth of their own minds.

Buddha, too, was one of these shramanas; even later, when he had become enlightened, he was still called "the Great Shramana," an epithet identical in meaning to "Mahamuni," that is, the great silent ascetic. Thus, he was considered one of those who followed the path of the pre-Aryan shramanas.

In addition to that, he was born in Kapilavastu, the city of Kapila, who was renowned as one of the greatest philosophers of the Sankhya system. Therefore it is likely that he became familiar early in his life with the teachings of the Sankhyas, a philosophy which forms the foundation of yoga and has many similarities with early Buddhism and Jainism.

Literally translated, Sankhya means "number, counting." It is one of the earliest scientific systems in the world. At the same time, it was also a science of life based on the polarity of different properties: If one unprejudicially enumerates different properties and qualities, one will recognize all kinds of opposites. If this has been acknowledged without bias, one will no longer try to force one's own ideas and ways of thinking on nature, but will carefully watch nature and learn by observation. But then one will also discover one's own polarity as it naturally is, and not according to our wishful thinking.

In this regard, Sankhya is a reality-oriented teaching which is very close to Buddhism, since it is not a theological system, but a system which leaves it open whether or not one is inclined to believe in a god. Such a belief is one's own private matter; one can believe in a god, but such a belief has nothing to do with reality. One has to understand the world as it is and to behave according to its rules, since it is impossible to oppose them. This is the reason why Buddha called his teaching "the eternal Dharma" *(sanatana-dharma)* or "the cosmic Dharma": the cosmic law which rules everything, whether we like it or not, whether we believe in it or deny it.

Some people may possibly believe that they can walk on water. But if they try, they will certainly sink into it. I remember one day a sadhu in Poona or Bombay made a big claim: On a certain day he would walk on water, because he was completely realized. Well, it may be that he really was completely realized, but when he tried to walk on water, he sank in and had to be dragged out. He had invited government cabinet members to his demonstration, and the audience had to pay a high admission fee which they demanded be returned when they saw him fall into the water. This is where "belief" can lead us! Belief is certainly a wonderful thing, but one should not try walking on water or overdo it otherwise.

26

Another sadhu announced in Bombay in a similar fashion that on a certain day he would let himself be entombed alive, and then he would rise up above his grave, soar into the sky, and disappear. Well, he was carried away in a goat chart. He never flew.

Today I am convinced that these people, and others who made similar claims, were honest and lovable human beings, full of faith and convinced of the truth of what they promised. And if somebody believes something which gives him strength, then this is great. But it is dangerous to believe in something which contradicts the laws of nature. This is why Buddha rejected all so-called "miracles." He did not endorse doing miracles in order to gain disciples. I know that there are some stories about "miracles" which Buddha is supposed to have performed, but all these stories are from a later time. According to the Pali canon, Buddha never performed any miracles, because he did not want to convince people with externals, but to let them experience the only miracle that really counts: the transformation of their minds. He was not interested in blindly believing adherents, but in convinced disciples.

This may be the main difference between religions that are based on a certain belief, and other religions, such as Buddhism, Jainism, Shramanism, and Taoism, which certainly encourage confidence based on conviction, but not on faithful acceptance. I do not know any other religion which is equally free of presuppositions and assumptions.

Therefore I wish to repeat: It is possible to believe in many things, as for example, in one's own body, the universe, the laws of the terrestrial bodies, or nature—all this is granted. But a belief has always to be in accord with what surrounds us, because it would be crazy to assume that the world would have developed over millions of years something that is unnecessary.

The world in which we live may be the product of our own imagination or a mere ideation which only appears to be the way in which we see it, without being so in reality, because our senses are limited. But nevertheless I am convinced that even our so-called illusions are not random: Even they are based on the laws of our psyche, and they in turn are part of the laws of the universe. Therefore we are the product of something which we do not really understand, and yet we have to respect it.

But now let's speak about one of the main differences between Hinduism and Buddhism. Let's remember the previously mentioned *advaita* philosophy of Shankaracharya, who lived around 800 A.D., and whose ideas many people think are identical with those of Buddhism.

Advaita means "non-duality." By this term Shankaracharya wanted to express that in reality only the "one"—the divine—is existent, and all multiplicity, diversity, and differences are nothing but an illusion. In other words, his *advaita* is a pure monism which, instead of acknowledging the illusion of multiplicity as being as true as the unity of all becoming (i.e., that both exist simultaneously), tried to concentrate only on the unity of all being. In order to perceive oneself as being different from illusion, his belief was based on transcending the illusion of differentiation. But since we are living in this illusory world, what can we do? It is as if somebody would decide not to dream— would such a decision free him from dreaming?

In Buddhism we have a term very similar to the Hindu *advaita*, but coined much earlier (about the first century A.D.), namely *advaya*. *Advaya* and *advaita* have two completely different meanings. While *advaita* means "the one without a second," *advaya*, "not two," points at transcending of any kind of duality: We may be under the spell of a certain illusion, but we realize that our illusion and its objects come from the same root. In other words we transcend the duality of the division into subject and object in the sense that we intuitively sense and realize that both emerge from the same cosmic ground.

Therefore the conception of *advaya* is completely contrary to the idea of *advaita*. And if people think—as nowadays happens frequently—that *advaita* is so similar to Buddhist ideas that they can be exchanged any-time, whereby one could follow Shankara's teachings as if they were Buddhist, then one does not do justice to either system. When Shankaracharya was accused during his lifetime of being a "crypto-Buddhist" because his teachings about maya had some external similarities to Mahayana teachings, he resolutely objected and even began accusing the Buddha of having been a great demagogue. He started a fierce attack on Buddhist ideas (which is still being continued by his followers), although he doubtlessly had incorporated essential ideas of Nagarjuna (who lived in the second century A.D. and emphasized the importance of emptiness).

And here it may be necessary to explain in a few words the Buddhist understanding of substance. Modern science demonstrates that there is no such thing as solid substance. Matter dissolves into different forces and becomes invisible. But between the pull of these forces there are huge empty spaces in about the same proportions as between the heavenly bodies in outer space. Thus, we soon have the impression that "matter" only very rarely occurs in the universe and that what we call "non-matter," or "space," is far more common than all "matter" taken together. But this means that "space" is the prerequisite for "matter" and that each and every thing emerges from "space." Everything else that exists is merely form, only differences in forms, or differences in accordance with the universal laws and forms of energy.

Therefore, if we talk about "matter," we have to keep in mind that it can be penetrated by radioactive energy as if there were no "density" at all. But our eyes, our sensing, our body are built in such a way that everything that we call "matter" offers resistance, and therefore we perceive it as "material." In reality, however, every piece of matter is nothing but a concentrated form of energy, and if we think of it as an accumulation of energy, then we begin to understand that "matter" is something more wonderful by far than all the wonders of the world.

If we hold a piece of wood in our hand, or a stone, or anything else, then we call it wood, stone, or something like that. But we do not realize what enormous energies are hidden in it. The power of an atom is so great that, if we understood the laws of nature, we could use it in either a beneficial or destructive way. These energies have always been present, but human beings did not know of their existence.

Lastly, here are a few comments on my theory that the teaching of karma is contradictory to the Vedic tradition and basically so different that one has to look for its origin in the shramana religions.

The famous Vedantic philosopher Yajnavalkya was one of the most outstanding thinkers in the Upanishads. In his philosophical ideas he did not strictly follow the Vedas, but maybe some of the Brahmanas, although he developed some visions which went far beyond their range. But he did not dare to talk about these new ideas, because he knew that if people really understood these new principles, they would do away with the entire Brahmanic philosophy.

Now it happened that one day a certain person was listening to Yajnavalkya talk about what happens when a human being dies. According to the Veda of the Brahmanic tradition, the eyes go to the sun, the hair into the trees and the grass, the blood into the water, the bones into the stones—in other words, everything returns to nature. And at this point this particular person asked, "What you are saying is very nice. But what happens to the human being? You did not say anything about him. You were talking only about his bodily components; but in a human being there are other principles working as well."

To this Yajnavalkya answered that he should keep his mouth shut; he would talk with him about it later, after the meeting. And what did they talk about? About karma! Thus, the teaching of karma was regarded as something so explosive and revolutionary that it was transmitted only to trusted disciples. This is because—as previously indicated—it made deities as well as sacrifices and worship superfluous. But without these the brahmins would have been jobless. They had always to emphasize the power of the yajna in order to continue to occupy the high rank they held within the Aryan social system. Even today they still make a living that way: When some years ago the conjunction of seven planets was imminent, they announced a catastrophic event for the whole world if great yajnas were not held in all of India. Provisions like wheat, rice, and butter were burned in great quantities, for millions of rupees, while the people went hungry. This is how deeply rooted the idea of yajna is in the Indian people even today!

Buddha was a good psychologist and therefore he avoided directly confronting the existing religious prejudices as long as they were not too obvious. He let everyone believe whatever he wanted. But he explained again and again that the only thing that really counted was what one does or does not. When one day somebody came up to him and implored him to teach him the path to Brahma, the highest creator god, Buddha agreed and asked that person whether he thought that Brahma was full of hatred.

"No," he replied, "he is full of love."

"Does he possess tendencies which we can so often observe in human beings: greed and ill will?"

"No, Lord, Brahma has only positive traits."

"Then go and cultivate those beneficial tendencies within yourself," Buddha said, "and your path will lead you to Brahma."

Thus he taught that faithful person, not by shocking him with the statement that there is no god or anything like that, but by encouraging him to realize his ideal, which he projected into a creator god endowed with these tendencies, within this lifetime—to become it himself.

But let's return once again to Shankaracharya—the great initiator of modern Hinduism. Above all, he attempted to rejuvenate the religious way of life of the Vedanta. Vedanta means "the end of the Vedas," because the Upanishads were originally at the end of the Vedas, and historically they really were the conclusion of that type of literature.

Without doubt Shankaracharya was an eminent scholar, whose ideas I respect a great deal without following them. His concern was to reform Brahmanism based on the most important Upanishads. From their perspective, that is from the perspective of *advaita*, he interpreted the Vedas. This is a wonderful interpretation, but it is not in accord with the basic ideas of those who created the Vedas. Therefore Shankaracharya's versions are certainly beautiful and appealing, but they do not correspond to history. This is because it is impossible to mix without a corresponding historical development something which was created in the sixth century B.C. with something else which was developed not before the sixth century A.D.

But the same is also true for Buddhism. If we want to understand it in its entirety, we have to study all its different aspects and see how they developed from budding nuclei, until we can finally embrace the total spectrum in its diversity. Then we can distill that which is necessary for our time, so that even today people can walk Buddha's path and Dharma.

In Tibet Padmasambhava was celebrated, and is still celebrated, as Buddha's reincarnation, because in the eighth century A.D. he gave the same teachings which Buddha Shakyamuni had propounded more than a thousand years ago in the language of his time. But Padmasambhava spoke in a form which could be understood and accepted by the people of Tibet. If Padmasambhava had used the same language, the same words, the same concepts as the Buddha did, he would hardly have been understood in Tibet. An exceptional man—an eminent scholar and an even greater psychologist who knew how to use the right means and to do it intentionally for the benefit of human beings—he was completely faithful to the *meaning* of the teachings, without clinging to externals. If we understand the essential aspects—not the externals—of his life and work, then we can learn from him how best to teach the Dharma in the West, here and now.

A Tibetan Buddhist
Looks at Christianity

Great religious and deep-rooted philosophical attitudes are not individual creations, though they may have been given their first impetus by great individuals. They grow from the germs of creative ideas, great experiences, and profound visions. They grow through many generations according to their own inherent law, just like a tree or any other living organism. They are what we might call "natural events of the spirit."

Foundations of Tibetan Mysticism

To understand a Tibetan Buddhist's attitude towards Christianity we must first of all know what religion means to him. The nearest Tibetan equivalent for "religion" is *chos* (Skt. *dharma*), which signifies the spiritual and universal law, the principle that supports *(dhar)* all that exists. To live in harmony with this law is the highest aspiration of man and means to dwell in a state of truth and virtue.

To a Tibetan, therefore, religion is not so much the adherence to a certain creed or dogma, but a natural expression of faith in the higher destiny of man, that is, in his capacity to free himself from the bondage of delusion and the narrowness of egohood in order to realize the universality of his true nature in the Enlightened Mind.

There are as many ways and methods to achieve this as there are types of human beings. Therefore, the Tibetan regards the diversity of religions not as a calamity or a reason for quarreling and mutual enmity, but as something that is natural and necessary for the spiritual growth of humanity.

The Tibetan, who is highly individualistic, therefore recognizes and respects innumerable forms of religious practice and devotion. Although there are many different schools of Buddhism in Tibet—as different from one another as the various Christian churches and sects—there is no enmity or sense of competition between them. They live peacefully side by side and recognize each other's validity. By accepting a teacher from one school one does not exclude those of other schools. Indeed, very often the teachings or methods of different schools complement and help each other in the most effective way.

The individualistic attitude in religious matters is expressed in a well-known Tibetan proverb:

Lung-pa re-re ka-lug re,
Lama re-re cho-lug re.
Every district has its own dialect,
Every Lama his own doctrine.

According to this principle, people are free to accept or to reject beliefs or practices according to their conviction and to express their opinions freely and fearlessly. Religious discussions are always welcomed, and people who can give convincing expression to their ideas are highly respected. The art of public discussion was particularly fostered by the big monastic universities like Ganden, Drepung, and Sera.

At the same time the Tibetan is not so naive as to believe that religious truths can be proved by mere logic or settled by arguments. Tibetan teachers always stress the fact that ultimate truth cannot be expressed in words, but only realized within ourselves. It is therefore not important what we believe, but what we experience and practice, and how it affects us and our surroundings. Whatever leads to a state of greater peace and harmony leads us on the right path.

In Tibet a saint is regarded more highly than a king, and a man able to renounce worldly possessions more highly than a rich man. A man who can sacrifice his own life out of love and compassion for his fellow-beings is honored more than a world conqueror.

Up to the present day the stories of the self-sacrificing career of the Buddha during innumerable previous lives on earth as a Bodhisattva are recounted at campfires, at religious and secular festivals, in homes and in hermitages, on lonely caravan-trails, and in crowded marketplaces. They never fail to stir the emotions of even the roughest mule-driver or the most sophisticated townsman, because these stories are not merely matters of a nebulous past, but have their counterparts in the lives of many Tibetan saints who have inspired past and present generations.

Under such circumstances it will be easy to understand that the story of Christ and his suffering on the cross for the sake of humanity is something that appeals deeply to the religious feelings of the average Tibetan. But if somebody would tell him, "Now you must abandon all other saints and saviors and only worship this one," he would be surprised and shocked at such a demand. For the Tibetan, the proof of truth lies in the very fact that at all times and among all peoples enlightened religious leaders and saints have appeared, who brought the message of love and compassion and reestablished the knowledge of that ultimate Reality, which Christians identify with God, Hindus with Brahman, and Buddhists with the state of Enlightenment, beyond words and definitions.

If Christianity could not make headway in Tibet, in spite of the warm reception which was accorded to early missionaries, then this had its reason not in a rejection of Christ or of his essential teachings but, on the contrary, in the fact that the teachings of Christ coincide with and are amply borne out by the Bodhisattva ideal and have been practiced in Tibet more than anywhere in Europe.

The second reason, however, was that those who tried to convey the teachings of Christ to Tibet were unwilling to recognize the great thoughts and saints of that country, and were more concerned with their own parochial outlook and man-made dogmas than with the universal message of Christ.

Nothing could illustrate better the Tibetan attitude towards Christianity than the following historical instances which amply bear out my contention.

The first Christian missionary to reach Tibet was the Portuguese Padre Antonio de Andrade, who in the year 1625 was received with great hospitality at Tsaparang by the king of Guge in Western Tibet. The king paid him high honor and, in the true spirit of Buddhist tolerance, allowed him to preach his religion! To him, a man who had traveled around half the world for the sake of his faith was certainly worth hearing and deserved the greatest respect.

He was convinced that truth cannot harm truth, and that, therefore, whatever was true in the religion of the stranger could only enhance, amplify, and bear out the teachings of Tibetan saints and of the Buddhas and Bodhisattvas. Was it not possible that in the countries of the West many a Bodhisattva had arisen, of whom the people of the East had not yet heard? So, out of the goodness of his heart, the king of Guge wrote the following letter to Padre Antonio de Andrade in the year 1625:

> We the King of the Kingdoms of Potente, rejoicing at the arrival in our lands of Padre Antonio Franguim (as the Portuguese were called in India) to teach us a holy law, take him for our Chief Lama and give him full authority to teach the holy law to our people. We shall not allow that anyone molest him in this, and we shall issue orders that he be given a site and all the help needed to build a house of prayer.

And the king gave even his own garden to the stranger, a gift which under the conditions of Tibet, where gardens are scarce and a rare luxury, was more than a mere polite gesture.

But, alas, the king in his unsuspecting goodness did not know that the stranger had come not merely to exchange true and beautiful thoughts with those who were striving after similar ideals, but to repudiate the teachings of Buddhism, in order to replace them with what he regarded as the sole truth. The conflict was inevitable: Discontent spread in the country, and the political opponents of the king rose against him.

While Padre Andrade, encouraged by his success in Tsaparang, proceeded to Lhasa in order to extend his activities over the whole of Tibet, a revolt broke out in Western Tibet, the king was overthrown, and with him the Guge dynasty and the glory of Tsaparang came to an end.

About a century later, in 1716, the Jesuit Padre Desideri arrived in Lhasa. He was given a beautiful house, provided with all the comfort of an honored guest, and was allowed to propagate his religion by preaching as well as through writing. In fact, he wrote a book in order to refute certain Buddhist teachings, which created much interest. This is how Desideri recorded the event:

> My home suddenly became the scene of incessant comings and goings by all sorts of people, chiefly learned men and professors, who came from the monasteries and universities, especially those of Sera and Drepung, the principal ones, to apply for permission to read the book.

Tibet in those days was certainly more civilized than contemporary Europe, where heretics and their books were burned and persecuted. One can imagine what would have happened in Rome if a stranger had tried to refute publicly the tenets of Christianity! No wonder, therefore, that the representatives of Christianity were not able to appreciate the spirit of tolerance and to take advantage of the door that was opened to them by reciprocating in the same spirit. Thus, the great opportunity was lost!

Yet, we may hope that when the followers of Christ and those of the Buddha meet again on the ground of mutual goodwill and understanding, there will come a day when the love which both Buddha and Christ preached so eloquently will unite the world in the common effort to save humanity from destruction by leading it towards the Light in which we all believe.

Siddhas and
Zen Buddhism

When religion grows in age, faith turns into dogma, and experience is replaced by book-knowledge, virtue by adherence to rules, devotion by ritual, meditation by metaphysical speculation. The time is now ripe for a rediscovery of truth and a fresh attempt to give it expression in life.

This is what happened in the sixth century B.C., when the Buddha revived Indian religious feeling through a reformulation of the ancient Dharma (for which the orthodox called him a revolutionary), and again a millennium later, when Buddhism had crystallized into so many philosophical schools and monastic institutions that the individual was in danger of getting lost in them, like a lone seafarer in the immensity of the ocean.

A new individualistic idealism sprang up then. It had its repercussions on the Chinese Ch'an School, which was called Zen in Japan, and on Indian Buddhist mystics whose records have been preserved in

Tibet in the stories of the eighty-four siddhas or "masters of the mystic path."

These siddhas, as well as the masters of the ancient Ch'an or Zen, were as revolutionary in their ideas and methods as the Buddha had seemed to the orthodox of his time. They were equally insistent that experience was more important than book-knowledge, and that "truth" could not be handed out in any "solid" or clearly definable (and therefore limited) form, in which it could be preserved for an indefinite time.

The Buddha discovered that it is not the results of human thought, the "ideas," beliefs and formulas, the conceptual knowledge, that matter, but the *method*, the spiritual *attitude* behind them. True to this fundamental principle, the Ch'an Buddhists in China and the siddhas in India refused to put their experiences into philosophical systems or to crystallize their ideas into doctrines.

They preferred the paradox to logical formulations and laid more stress on the spirit of inquiry than on solutions. Their spiritual attitude was expressed in one word—shunyata. Shunyata literally means "emptiness," but this term has many gradations of meaning. In the present instance it may be interpreted as complete absence of prejudice and preconceived ideas. It is the intuitive state of mind, which in the Indian system of meditation is called *dhyana* and from which the word Ch'an or Zen is derived.

There are as many ways of achieving this as there are thinking beings. So each of the masters developed his own method and—what is more—made each of his pupils find his own particular way. This is what makes it so difficult to give a precise idea of what Zen or the siddhas stand for, without overstressing individual aspects or oversimplifying the problem by mere generalization.

They did not believe in verbal expressions of truth, and only pointed out the direction in which truth might be experienced, since truth is not something existing in itself, not even as a negation of error, as Joka, a pupil of the Patriarch Eno (638–713 A.D.), sings in his hymn *Shodo-Ka:*

I do not seek the truth,
I do not destroy the error,
Because I know that both are nothing,
That both are no forms (of reality),
The Unformed is nevertheless not "nothing,"
But also not "Not-nothing."

And in the same hymn we find the words: "The empty shape of transitory illusion is nothing but the shape of truth." Tagore expresses a similar idea when he says: "If you close your doors against all errors, you exclude the truth."

All our logical definitions are one-sided and partial, since they are bound to their starting point: the judging intellect and the particular angle of vision. What people generally regard as truth is little more than a one-sided statement.

A fine example of this is the story of two Chinese monks who had a dispute about a flag moving in the wind. The one maintained that the flag was moving; the other, that it was the wind that moved. Eno (Hui-Neng), the Sixth Patriarch in China, who overheard their discussion, said: "Neither the wind nor the flag is moving; your mind moves."

But Mummon, a Japanese Patriarch of the thirteenth century, not satisfied with this answer, went one step further and said: "Neither the wind, nor the flag, nor the mind is moving," thus going back to the ultimate principle of shunyata, in which there is neither going nor coming, comprising both the subjective and objective aspects of reality.

The reality beyond the opposites, however, is not to be separated or abstracted from its exponents; the momentariness is not to be distinguished from eternity. The most perfect individual self-expression is the most objective description of the world. The greatest artist is he who expresses what is felt by everybody. But how does he do it?—By being more subjective than others. The more he expresses *himself*, the nearer he comes to the others, because our real nature is not our imaginary, limited ego. Our true nature is vast, all-comprehensive, and intangible as empty space. It is shunyata in its deepest sense.

Clear and unimpaired is the light of the spiritual
    mirror,
Boundlessly penetrating the innumerable realms,
Which are as countless as the sands of the sea.
In its center there is formed as a picture the whole
    world.
It is a perfect light; it is unbroken:
It is neither merely inside nor outside.

Shodo-Ka

It is the secret of art that it reveals the supra-indi-
vidual through individuality, the "not-self" through
the "self," the object through the subject. Art in itself
is a sort of paradox, and that is why Zen escapes from
the dilemma of logical limitation, of partiality and one-
sidedness. It cannot be bound down to principles or
conceptual definitions, because it exaggerates intentionally, and a literal interpretation is not possible. Its
meaning is beyond the incongruity of words.

Paradoxes, like humor, are greatly dependent on
the soil in which they grow. Thus there is a marked
difference between the paradoxes which we find in
the stories of the Indian Buddhist siddhas and those
of the Zen masters in China and Japan. In the stories
of the Siddhas, the paradoxes take either the form of
the miraculous, in which inner experiences are symbolized, or they show that the very thing by which a
man falls can be the cause of his rise, that a weakness
can be turned into strength, a fault into an asset, if
only we were able to look at ourselves, like a stranger,

without bias and prejudice, and upon the world around us, as if we had never seen it before.

We are blind to reality, because we are so accustomed to our surroundings and to ourselves that we are no more aware of them. Once we break the fetters of habit by the power of a paradoxical situation or by a flash of intuition, everything becomes a revelation and everyday life turns into a wonder. In the stories of the tantric mystics, the wondrous experience which follows the great spiritual change is symbolized by miracles and extraordinary psychic powers *(siddhi)*. In Zen Buddhism with its refined psychology, the scene of activity is entirely located in the human mind and the paradoxes are of a more complex nature.

Perhaps it was this difference in treatment and style which prevented scholars up to now from recognizing the inner relationship between Zen masters and siddhas, though thousands of miles and hundreds of years may have separated them.

The following story, which might be aptly entitled "The man who met with himself," may serve as an example. It is found in the Tibetan biographies of the eighty-four siddhas *(Grub-thob brgyad-cu-rtsa-bzhi'i-rnam-thar)*, who flourished between the seventh and the eleventh centuries.

The story runs as follows: There was once a hunter, called Savari. He was very proud of his strength and his marksmanship. The killing of animals was his sole occupation, and it made his life one single sin.

One day, while he was out hunting, he saw a stranger approaching him from afar, apparently a hunter. "Who dares hunt in my territory?" he thought indignantly, and walking up, he found that the stranger was not only as big and sturdy as himself, but—what surprised him still more—he looked exactly like himself! "Who are you?" he demanded sternly.

"I am a hunter," said the stranger, unperturbed.

"Your name?"

"Savari."

"How is that?" the hunter exclaimed, taken aback. "My name is also Savari! Where do you come from?"

"From a distant country," the stranger said, evading the question.

Savari regained his self-confidence.

"Can you kill more than one deer with the shot of a single arrow?"

"I can kill three hundred with one shot," the stranger answered. This sounded to Savari like tall talk, and he wished only for an opportunity to expose his rival's ridiculous claim.

However, the stranger—no other than the Bodhisattva Avalokiteshvara, who had assumed this shape because he felt pity for Savari—immediately created a herd of five hundred deer through his magic

Mahasiddha Savari

power. Savari was delighted when he saw the deer emerge from the forest at not too great a distance, and he asked gleefully: "Will your arrow be able to go through all those deer?"

"It will go through all five hundred," the stranger replied, but Savari suggested: "Let your arrow miss four hundred and kill one hundred only."

The stranger accomplished this feat with the greatest ease, but now Savari began to disbelieve his eyes.

"Fetch one of the deer," said the stranger, "if you have any doubt." And Savari did as he was told.

But, alas! When he tried to lift one of the deer, he found it so heavy that he could not move it from the spot.

"What?" exclaimed the stranger, "you, a great hunter, cannot even lift a single deer!" And he laughed heartily.

Now the hunter's pride was completely broken. He fell at the stranger's feet and asked him to be his teacher.

Avalokiteshvara agreed. "If you want to learn this magic shooting art," he said, "you must first purify yourself for a month by not eating meat and by meditating on love and compassion towards all living beings. I will then return and teach you my secret."

Savari did as he was told, and when the teacher returned, he was a changed man, though he did not know this yet. He asked the Guru for his promised initiation into the secret art of shooting.

The teacher drew an elaborate mandala (a concentric diagram, used as an aid in meditation), decorated it with flowers and told Savari and his wife to look at it carefully.

Since both of them had seriously practiced meditation for one full month, they gazed with undivided attention upon the mandala, and lo!—the ground below it seemed to become transparent, and it was as though they looked right into the bowels of the earth. There was smoke and fire, and agonizing shrieks pierced their ears.

"What do you see?" asked the Guru.

The hunter and his wife were unable to utter a word. But when the smoke had cleared away, they saw the eight great hells and the agony of innumerable human beings.

"What do you see?" the Guru asked again.

And when they looked closer, they recognized two painfully contorted faces.

"What do you see?" the Guru asked for the third time.

And suddenly, full comprehension came over them like a flash, and they cried out: "It's ourselves!"

They fell at the feet of the Guru, imploring him to show them the way of liberation. But they entirely forgot to ask for the initiation into the secret shooting art.

Savari continued to meditate on love and compassion and became one of the eighty-four siddhas.

It is interesting and instructive to see the main features of this story in the garb of Zen, as related in Chuan-teng Lu.[1]

Shih-kung was a hunter before he was ordained as a Zen monk under Ma-tsu. He strongly disliked Buddhist monks, who were against his profession. One day, while chasing a deer, he passed by the cottage where Ma-tsu resided. Ma-tsu came out and greeted him.

Shih-kung asked: "Did you see some deer pass by your door?"

"Who are you?" asked the master.

"I am a hunter."

"How many can you shoot down with your arrow?"

"One with one arrow."

"Then you are no hunter," declared Ma-tsu.

"How many can you shoot with one arrow?" asked the hunter in his turn.

"The entire flock, with one arrow."

"They are living creatures, why should you destroy the whole flock at one shooting?"

"If you know that much, why don't you shoot yourself?"

"As to shooting myself, I do not know how to proceed."

54

"This fellow," exclaimed Ma-tsu, all of a sudden, "has put a stop today to all his past ignorance and evil passions!"

Thereupon, Shih-kung the hunter broke his bow and arrows and became Ma-tsu's pupil.

When he became a Zen master himself, he had a bow with an arrow ready to shoot, with which his monks were threatened when they approached him with a question.

Shih-ping was once so treated. Shih-kung exclaimed: "Look out for the arrow!"

Ping opened his chest and said: "This is the arrow that kills; where is the one that resuscitates?"

Kung struck three times on the bow-string. Ping made a bow. Kung said: "I have been using one bow and two arrows for the past thirty years, and today I have succeeded in shooting down only a half of a wise man."

Shih-kung broke his bow and arrows once more, and never used them again.

Notes

1. D. T. Suzuki, *Essays on Zen Buddhism,* Second Series (Boston: The Beacon Press, 1952), p. 97 (author's paraphrase).

Part Two

AWAKENING VISION

Meditation, Mudra,
and Mandala

The Tibetan pantheon of deities originated from the Buddha as the embodiment of all human and divine qualities, and from people meditating upon these qualities and the ideal of Buddhahood. The Buddha represents the complete human being. To look upon him as a kind of deity would not be of great help to us. If we realize that the Buddha is, or was, a human being like ourselves who attained the completeness of his nature that we call enlightenment, then we can understand the Buddha in symbolic form as the ideal of what we want to realize within ourselves.

The Buddha went through many different experiences in his lifetime. At first he struggled, trying to find the solution to the riddles of life through asceticism and severe practices. When he found that self-mortification did not lead to enlightenment, he gave up these extreme practices which had brought him to the threshold of death, again took normal food, and after having regained his strength, he went into a deep state of meditation. Finally, he came through intense inner struggle to the point of enlightenment. Not content at having attained his own liberation, he renounced the blissful state of peace and happiness which he enjoyed in the solitude of the forest, and returned to the world in order to bring liberation to all who are in the bondage of ignorance and delusion. Having initially revealed his teachings in a sermon at Sarnath, he continued to help people for over forty years, teaching them how to meditate, how to find a way out of the suffering of this life.

All these various qualities and activities of the Buddha are represented in various mudras, which are symbolic hand and body positions depicted in art. Sometimes we see the Buddha in the earth-touching mudra, sometimes in the mudra of giving, the mudra of meditating, or the mudra of teaching. Each of these mudras represents a particular spiritual attitude, a particular aspect of the Buddha's wisdom.

The earth-touching gesture signifies the Wisdom of the Great Mirror in which things are seen in their true nature *(yatha-bhutam)*. It is also the gesture in which the Buddha called the earth as witness of his past acts of renunciation, in which his own nature as an enlightened being is revealed. The gesture of giving signifies the Wisdom of the Essential Equality of all living beings. The gesture of meditation signifies the Wisdom of Distinguishing Inner Vision. The gesture of fearlessness (blessing) symbolizes the All-Accomplishing Wisdom, and the gesture of teaching or Setting in Motion the Wheel of the Dharma signifies the Dharmadhatu Wisdom of Transcendental Knowledge.

When these different activities of the Buddha are seen as different states of consciousness which the Enlightened One reveals, each becomes a separate symbol—a separate Buddha. Thus, the plurality of Buddhas only expresses the many facets of Buddhahood. For instance, although white light consists of many qualities in the form of colors, they are not seen until light passes through a prism. Then the whole spectrum of reds, blues, and yellows shines forth. At that moment, you realize that all this is contained in white light, even though you never noticed it before.

In the same way, when you see the various Buddha forms, they only represent the many qualities of the Buddha mind. All these qualities are actually, or potentially, within us. This is the origin of the many different Buddhas. They are not intentionally created fabrications, but arise from within the meditation. Different schools of Buddhism and individual teachers specialized in developing these various qualities, and thus many pantheons arose. All these symbols and deities and mandalas are really the products of meditational experiences through the millenniums.

When you look at a Tibetan painting of a deity, you see auras: Every Buddha has a halo around his head and another around his body. To some extent, the head aura indicates whether the spiritual attitude is active or passive, and is often green, red, or orange. An aura of flames indicates another kind of activity. Such awe-inspiring forms as Vajrapani or Mahakala are often called "wrathful deities," but they, too, are manifestations of this same Buddha-energy. They are frightening for the simple reason that we are afraid of anything we don't understand. Thus, these deeper aspects of the Buddha's knowledge are represented in these seemingly fearful forms.

The significance of the flaming aura is often mis-understood in the West, because Christian iconography associates a halo of flames with hell. Therefore, people tend to assume that any figure surrounded by flames must be a kind of demon. In Buddhism, how-ever, it is quite the opposite. They are not demons—rather, they are embodiments of wisdom. Flames fittingly symbolize the penetrating quality of higher wisdom, for they burn away all obstructing impurities, melting and integrating them into one brilliant form of energy.

Bodily auras—particularly a very dark blue one encircling the figure—also symbolize shunyata or infinite space. In special thankas, this blue is broken by intricate golden rays. These rays are never straight, but always curved, accurately paralleling the discover-ies of modern physics that indicate everything in the universe moves in curves and there is no straight move-ment. Meditators intuitively realized what scientists later verified through mathematical formulas. Further-more, these fine rays sometimes alternate between plain and wavy lines, vibrating, as it were, on a longer or shorter frequency. This relates to a certain mantric science in which it is said there are four different types of mantras, represented by four different vibrations and resulting in four different effects.

This should give you some introduction to the ico-nography of Tibetan art. It must be remembered that all these iconographic forms originated in meditation and that, therefore, most of the symbols crystallized out of the various methods of meditation represent archetypal expressions of the human psyche. As we are all human beings with the same structure, we can communicate with the same symbols. Otherwise there would be no way to communicate at all. The human psyche is not just a mixture of anything and every-thing, nor is it something formless and completely anarchical. Rather, it reveals a very definite structure. Thousands of people through thousands of years com-bined their efforts in exploring this structure, and slowly some experiences crystallized. When these crystallizations are artistically represented, they pro-vide us with a path to the same realization.

Entering the Realm of the Sacred: Buddhist Art and Architecture

Art is the living expression of religion. Religion without art is a dead system of dogmas which have no effect on life. As long as Buddhism was reduced to the narrow confines of a monastic community, it exhausted itself in dogmatic quarrels and discussions which had no effect on the lay-community, but with the advent of Mahayana Buddhism the greatest works of art in India were created, and Buddhism spread its message over the greater part of Asia.

This was all the more remarkable as it was not due to force of arms or to the power of economics, but to the creative faculty of its cultural impact which stimulated the dormant genius of various peoples, and created a burst of artistic activity in the form of architecture, sculpture, painting, poetry, and ritual music. On the popular level the Jatakas (birth stories of the Buddha) excited the imagination of the common man and made him feel one with all living creatures, while the Bodhisattva-ideal made him a participant in the quest for truth and liberation. It gave him hope and confidence to follow the Buddha's way and to strive after the highest aim, which up to then had been unobtainable in its remoteness and superhuman qualities.

It is a fallacy to say that the Buddha was deified in the Mahayana in opposition to a strictly human personality in early Buddhism. In the early schools of Buddhism the Buddha's position was so elevated that no being, human or god, could hope to attain it.

There is a story: The Buddha was once sitting in deep meditation at the roots of a tree in the midst of the forest. A hunter approached the immobile and luminous figure of the Buddha and asked him: "Are you a tree spirit?" The Buddha answered, "No." "Are you perhaps a god?" the hunter continued, and the Buddha again answered, "No." "Are you a man then?" he ventured, but the Buddha answered, "I am the Enlightened One, the teacher of gods and men, the Buddha who has left behind him both realms!" Even the gods were mortals, who had to become human again in order to be released from the law of karma that had temporarily freed them from want and suffering.

The Buddha was regarded as being superior to the gods, and was therefore called "the god of gods" (Skt. *devadevanan*). It was possible for a man to be reborn in the realm of gods if he lived a godly life. Even the

Buddha had declared this when he explained that the way to Brahma consisted in a life in which the divine qualities attributed to Brahma were realized. But it was regarded as presumptuous to strive after Buddha-hood, which was so exceptional a state that even the gods regarded it beyond their powers to attain. In the present *kalpa* (a world-cycle of astronomical length and of almost unimaginable duration) only five Enlightened Ones, only five Buddhas, were thought to be possible, while other *kalpas* were even less favorable, if not altogether barren of Buddhas.

Therefore the Arhat was regarded as the highest ideal that could be attained by a man if he was earnest in his endeavor. This was the ideal of the saint, who liberated himself without being able to liberate others, because his saintliness consisted in avoiding evil and temptation and in practicing renunciation, without having the universal knowledge of the Dharma and the power to reveal it to others.

The Mahayana, however, rejected this ideal because the Arhat's liberation consisted merely in the overcoming of individual suffering by the total extinction of life, while a Buddha was able to attain perfect enlightenment even in his human body, and thus benefit all living beings. If this were possible, then everybody should strive for this, whether it would be attainable in one or in many lives. After all, we have an eternity of time before us, and we can lose nothing by attempting to strive after the highest ideal.

Originally the Arhat, the Pratyekabuddha (the solitary Enlightened One who was not endowed with the capacity to teach the Dharma), and the Samyaksambuddha, the Fully Enlightened One, seemed to be models for the classification of three types of human beings. But in the time of King Kanishka (first century A.D.), they were regarded as ideals of religious life, and from this point of view there could be no doubt that the ideal of the Fully Enlightened One was the highest one. Therefore, in each school of Buddhism adherents of the great (Mahayana) as well as of the lesser Vehicle (Hinayana) can be found. One thing seems fairly clear in this yet unresolved problem, namely that Fa-hian and Hsüan-tsang, whose chronicles brought this distinction into prominence, have given the Chinese versions of the terms Mahayana and Hinayana to institutions which they recognized as such, either by first-hand observation or by hearsay, institutions which in Buddhaghosha's school were known under quite different designations.

The extension of the name Mahayana was, and is, of a vague and fluid kind. Those to whom it was applied formed no closed unit. And this is true of most of the so-called "sects." They frequently overlapped in their heretical views.[1]

Only by the strictly conservative members of the Theravadins and other similarly "orthodox" sects was it regarded to be presumptuous to strive after Buddhahood.

Those to whom Buddhism was not only a dogma but a conviction of the heart regarded it as selfish to strive after one's personal liberation only, without the capacity or the possibility of sharing it with others. Thus Buddhahood was no more regarded as an unapproachable, unique state of mind, but as something attainable by every human being who made the required effort. In this way, the Buddha became an example for every individual, instead of being an unattainable ideal. He became the very essence and hope of humanity, irrespective of caste, creed, sex, or nationality.

This was a new thing in ancient India, where religion and caste were bound by the soil. Thus Buddhism became the first messenger of Indian culture in foreign countries. This was not achieved through wars or weapons or through political superiority or economic pressure, but by convincing others of the truth of the Dharma.

The exalted state of the Buddha was not diminished but brought nearer to those who felt in harmony with his teachings. Even if the Buddha possessed divine qualities, these did not separate him from his followers, who were convinced that those qualities were inherent in all living beings and needed only to be developed in order to realize enlightenment. In India the human and divine properties were never as sharply divided as in the West, a fact that was never sufficiently realized by Western scholars who were of the opinion that the Buddha had been deified in the Mahayana in contrast to his human origin. They unconsciously projected the Christian idea of God into the terminology of Buddhism, where men can become gods and gods can become men, according to their karma or their spiritual development. The divine qualities of the Buddha are Wisdom and Compassion, but no real Buddhist would hold him responsible for the creation of the world, which is a unique feature of the biblical idea of God. In order to understand the historical and spiritual development of Buddhism, we have to admit that the conception of Buddhahood changed from an unapproachable, quasi-transcendental state to an exalted but attainable ideal.

In some of the first great monuments in memory of the Buddha, the overawed community did not dare to portray the Buddha in human form, but rather symbolized his presence by showing his footprints in the form of lotuses or depicting his empty throne.

The first reaction against the extreme deification of the Buddha which tried to separate him from his most devoted followers was a personification of his image in the form of a human portrayal which, in the colonial art of Gandhara, often bordered on the trivial. Though there are exceptions to the rule, the bulk of the Gandhara art was a poor imitation of Greek sculpture and gave more prominence to the folds of the robe than to the character of the face. But, fortunately, the indigenous spirit of devotion soon resulted in a more genuine art which no more endeavored to portray any particular human being but tried to express serenity, peace, and inner happiness as the main characteristics of an Enlightened One.

The images of the Buddha assumed more and more expressions of inwardness, of states of profound meditation, enlightenment, and equanimity. There was something exalted and noble in all of them, but it was the nobility of wisdom and compassion which even nowadays moves and inspires us, whether we are religious-minded or not. There is something that is both human and divine, something that touches our heart, as no otherworldly power, no almighty world creator could have done. Even when these images had become stylized and conventional, they evoked memories of qualities and lofty ideals, like ciphers of an ancient language, reminding us of past achievements.

Notes

1. Shwe Zan Aung and Caroline Rhys Davids, trans., *Points of Controversy* (Henley-on-Thames, England: Pali Text Society), pp. 45–46.

The Eight Forms of Guru Padmasambhava

Guru Padmasambhava was invited to Tibet by King Trisong Detsen in the year 747 A.D., where he established the first Buddhist monastery at Samye in 787, and founded the oldest school of Buddhism in Tibet, known as Nyingma. He was one of the greatest scholars and masters of yoga of his time. He acquired the knowledge and practice of all the major sadhanas and yogic methods of tantric and pre-tantric times, and he received initiation into eight fundamental doctrines.

The eight forms in which Padmasambhava is depicted are therefore not different incarnations, as popularly believed, but the representations of his eight main initiations, in each of which he assumed a new personality, symbolized by a new name (as gained in higher forms of initiation), and a form of appearance corresponding to that name. Because initiation is equivalent to entering a new life, it is a form of rebirth.

Guru Padmasambhava

In his most important and characteristic form Guru Padmasambhava appears in the royal robes of the king of Zahor, but holding the insignia of spiritual realization.

1. The *khatvanga*, a staff, surmounted by a double-vajra *(vishvavajra)*, the symbol of universality and the "Wisdom that Accomplishes All Works"; a vessel containing the elixir of immortality (Skt. *amrita-kalasha*); and two human heads and a skull, symbolizing greed, hatred, and ignorance, which have been overcome by the knowledge of the Three Worlds and the Three Times, symbolized by a flaming trident *(trishula)*. The staff itself represents the *sushumna* or the central current of psychic energy, which combines the solar and lunar forces *(pingala* and *ida,* respectively) in one mighty uprush of conscious realization. Thus, all these symbols constitute various aspects of insight into the nature of reality.

2. The skull-bowl *(kapala)*, in which the vessel with the elixir of immortality is placed, rests in the left hand of the Guru, because the knowledge or conscious experience of death (as gained in the higher forms of initiation) leads to the realization of immortality, to the experience of the Greater Life. The elixir of immortality is the attribute of Amitayus, the Buddha of Infinite Life, the Sambhogakaya reflex of the Dhyani-Buddha Amitabha.

3. The Vajra in the Guru's right hand (raised in *abhaya-mudra,* the gesture of fearlessness and blessing) is the

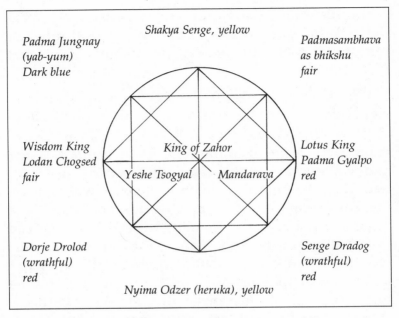

Mandala of the eight forms of Padmasambhava

scepter of spiritual power, the means through which wisdom is put into action. It may also be displayed in a threatening attitude, the hand above the right knee, in the act of subduing evil forces. In a devotional Tibetan text Padmasambhava is described in the following words:

> Being the end of confusion and the beginning of realization,
> He wears the royal robes of the Three Vehicles (of liberation),

74

He holds the Vajra of Skillful Means in his right
hand
And in his left the Skull-bowl of Wisdom with the
Elixir of Life.
He cuts off the heads of hatred, greed, and
ignorance
And carries them like ornaments on his trident.

His hat (known as the "lotus cap") is adorned with
the symbols of the crescent moon, the sun-disk, and
a small flame-like protuberance, which signifies the
union of lunar and solar forces (Tib. *thig-le*), the realization of the Dharmadhatu wisdom. The hat is surmounted by a vajra and an eagle's feather. The latter
indicates the Guru's soaring mind, penetrating the
highest realms of reality.

Flanking the main figure of Padmasambhava are
two female devotees. Evans-Wentz identifies the two
figures as Bhasadhara, the queen of Zahor, and the
Princess Mandarava. But since Padmasambhava left
the royal palace and gave up his kingdom, like Buddha
Shakyamuni before him, Bhasadhara, to whom he had
been married, did not play any further role in his life.
However, the two female devotees and disciples who
were of paramount importance were the Indian Princess Mandarava and the Tibetan Khadroma Yeshe
Tsogyal. Both of them are looked upon as reincarna-
tions of divine origin. The latter, who was regarded as
an incarnation of Sarasvati, the goddess of learning,
was gifted with such a perfect memory that she was

able to remember the Guru's every word. In this way she became Padmasambhava's sole biographer. Iconographically she is shown in the garb of a heavenly being of white complexion, adorned with the traditional ornaments and flying scarves, while Mandarava is generally clad in the costume of an Indian hill-princess. Her face is of yellowish complexion. Both devotees are depicted in the act of offering *amrita* (nectar) either from a skull-bowl or a vase-like vessel.

Over the head of Padmasambhava often appears the red Dhyani-Buddha Amitabha, the Buddha of Infinite Light. He is the spiritual source of Padmasambhava, who thus may be called an embodied ray of Amitabha on the earthly plane.

Therefore, in the dedicatory verses at the beginning of the Bardo Thodol (Tib. *Bar-do'i thos-grol*), the Book of the Spontaneous Liberation from the Intermediate State (between life and rebirth) known as "The Tibetan Book of the Dead" and ascribed to Padmasambhava, it is said:

To Amitabha (the Buddha of) Infinite Light, as
    Dharmakaya (the Body of the Universal Law),
To the peaceful and wrathful forms (of the
    Dhyani-Buddhas) of the Lotus Order,
    as Sambhogakaya (the Body of Spiritual
    Enjoyment),
To Padmasambhava, the Protector of Sentient

Beings, as human incarnation (Nirmanakaya,
Body of Transformation):
Obeisance to them the Gurus of the Three Bodies.

Sun and moon, seen in the upper space of every
thanka, represent the spiritual forces of *pingala* and *ida*,
which move the universe and flow as two currents of
energy through the human body.

Grouped around the main image of Guru
Padmasambhava, who forms the center of the ninefold
mandala, are his eight forms of appearance:

1. Padma Jungnay (Tib. *Padma-'byung-gnas*, "the
Lotus-born," Skt. Padmasambhava) in his Vajrasattvic
form, dark blue, embraced by his *Prajna*, the embodiment of his Wisdom (generally light blue, sometimes
white), because—according to his symbolical biography—Padmasambhava took on the aspect of
Vajradhara when he was initiated into the doctrine of
the Great Perfection (Tib. *rDzogs-chen*), in which the
indestructible and transparent diamond-nature of our
innermost being is realized.

2. Guru Shakya Senge (Tib. *Shakya-seng-ge*, "The Lion
of the Shakya Clan"). In this form Padmasambhava is
identified with Shakyamuni, the historical Buddha,
thus indicating Padmasambhava's initiation into the
teachings of the earliest schools of Buddhism, as represented by the Small Vehicle (Hinayana).

3. Guru Padmasambhava as a *bhikshu* or pandit of the
Great Vehicle, indicating his initiation into the teach-

ings of the Mahayana School and his entering upon the Bodhisattva Path.

4. Guru Lodan Chogsed (Tib. *Blo-ldan-mchog-sred*), the "Guru Possessing Wisdom and the Highest Aspirations." He appears here in kingly robes, his right hand raised with a *damaru*, from which the eternal sound *(shabda)* of the Dharma rhythmically emerges and pervades the universe. The left hand holds a skull-bowl brimming with the elixir of immortality.

5. Guru Padma Gyalpo (Tib. *Padma-rgyal-po*, "the Lotus King"), is very similar to the previous figure; he distinguishes himself mainly by holding the Mirror of Truth in his left hand. Sometimes he is also depicted with the mirror held up in his right hand, in which case the left hand holds the skull-bowl. In some thankas the emblems of these two kings are reversed, so that it seems these two figures are more or less interchangeable.

6. Guru Dorje Drolog (Tib. *rDo-rje-gro-lod*), "the Diamond Comforter," manifests in a wrathful appearance *(krodha-bhairava)*, red in color, surrounded by flames (symbolizing knowledge in its "terrible" illusion-devouring aspect), riding on a tiger, holding a vajra in his outstretched right hand, and in his left hand a *phur-bu*, a magical dagger which destroys evil influences, exorcises demons, and drives away the powers of darkness. The prostrate human form underneath the tiger represents a conquered demon.

7. Guru Nyima Odzer (Tib. *Nyi-ma-'od-zer*), "the Sun-ray Guru," appears as an ascetic of the Heruka (unclad) type. His left (sometimes his right) hand holds the sun by a ray, his right (sometimes his left) hand holds a three-pointed staff (Skt. *khatvanga*). He wears a crown of skulls and a tiger-skin around his loins. His color is yellow.

8. Guru Senge Dradog (Tib. *Senge-ge-sgra-sgrogs*), "the Guru with the Roaring Voice of a Lion," is a dark blue demoniacal figure, clad in a lion-skin dangling from his shoulders and a tiger-skin as a loin-cloth. He is surrounded by flames; in his right hand he wields a vajra in a menacing way, and the left hand is either empty or holds a bell before his chest. He stands on the bodies of two conquered demons.

The Mandala of the
Dhyani-Buddhas

There is an ancient language retained in the different mudras or gestures of the Buddha. They are symbols of the different stages of spiritual development
through which he went, and this development is what
every true Buddhist has to go through, if he is striving
for ultimate liberation and enlightenment.

Thus it happened that even in the earliest monu-
ment of Buddhism known to us, people were not
content merely to preserve the relics of the Buddha in
a magnificent stupa, but they made it a center of worship by providing a path of circumambulation, en-
closed by a stone-railing with four gates that mark the
four most important events in the Buddha's life. The
eastern gate symbolizes his birth, the southern gate
(which also marks the sun's zenith) his enlightenment,
the western gate his first sermon at Isipathana, and
the northern gate his final Parinirvana. They compared the Buddha, whose relics were enshrined either
in the center of the stupa or on its summit, with the

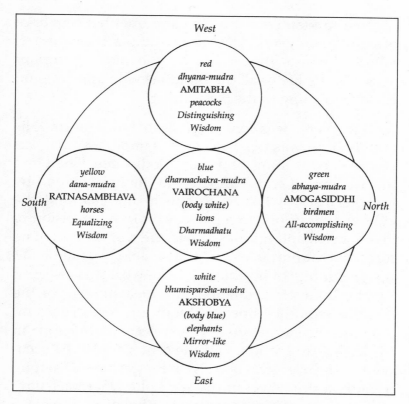

Mandala of the Dhyani-Buddhas

spiritual sun, whose rays illuminate the world, while those who received its rays moved like planets around the sun of the *pradakshina-patha*, the path of circumambulation, from left to right.

Thus the first mandala was created, which became a model for all subsequent mandalas, though they were perfected and refined in many ways. What became fundamental was the sun-oriented sequence of significant events in the life of Buddha Shakyamuni, whose life was the model for the most important stages in the life of all the Buddhas who appeared on earth (according to the Scriptures).

But there was one significant difference. His earthly birth was regarded as less important than his spiritual awakening under the Bodhi-tree. Therefore his awakening was compared to the illumination by the first rays of the rising sun in the east and the culmination of his career was seen in his decision to give himself and his message to the world, though he foresaw that only a few would be able to understand the profundity of his doctrine. The west was reserved for the hour of meditation in which the eye of the Dharma would be opened; the north would be compared to the Parinirvana or the release from karma in the karma-free action, and the center would be occupied by the universal Buddha in the gesture of "setting in motion the wheel of the law," the Dharmachakra, which has become the central symbol of Buddhism.

These five attitudes in the life of the historical Buddha correspond to the meditative experience of Buddhahood in the form of the five Jinas or Dhyani-Buddhas: Akshobhya in the east of the mandala, Ratnasambhava in the south, Amitabha in the west, Amoghasiddhi in the north, and Vairochana in the center. They are distinguished by their color, their gesture (mudra), and their throne-bearer *(vahan)*.

Dhyani Buddha Vairochana

Their colors correspond to the directions of the sky and to the rays of the sun: white in the hour before sunrise in the east; yellow in the zenith (south), red at sunset, dark green at midnight (north), and blue in the center. Blue and white are interchangeable in certain cases.

Even more important are the gestures (mudra). The first is the earth-touching gesture of Akshobhya in the east; the second is the gesture of giving *(dana-mudra)*, in which the palm of Ratnasambhava is turned outside, the back of the hand resting on the right knee. The third is the gesture of meditation of Amitabha in the west, and the fourth is the gesture of reassurance ("don't fear!") of Amoghasiddhi in the north. In the center sits Vairochana (the sun-Buddha) in the gesture of turning the wheel of the universal law.

In order to distinguish Shakyamuni Buddha from Akshobhya, who displays the same gesture as the historical Buddha (and is sometimes shown in a gilded metal-image), we have to observe the throne-animal, which in the case of Akshobhya is the white elephant, and in the case of Shakyamuni, the deer (because he delivered his first sermon in the Deer Park of Isipathana). The *vahan* of Ratnasambhava is the horse, the symbol of liberation, because the Buddha left his home on a horse; the *vahan* of Amitabha is the peacock (to symbolize the colorful rays of the sinking sun), while the vehicle of Amoghasiddhi in the north is a mythical figure half man, half bird, symbolizing the transition from the human to the superhuman state, which takes place in the mysterious darkness of the night, invisible to the eye.

The functions of these Dhyani-Buddhas, who are immanent as well as transcendent in so far as they transcend objective and limited existence, are clearly expressed in their gestures. They are an expression of those four attitudes of the mind which, like the four parts of a symphony, end in a grand finale in which they all merge and find their unity or universal completeness in the center of the mandala, the wisdom of the Dharma-sphere.

Of the four "movements" that lead to the center, the first is the Wisdom of the Great Mirror in which we see the world as it is *(yatha-bhutam)* and our own position in it. Therefore it is expressed in the gesture of touching the ground, the firm basis on which we stand and which is at the same time the totality of our past. The second Wisdom, expressed in the gesture of giving of Ratnasambhava, is the Wisdom of the Essential Equality of Beings, as they all have the same origin.

The third attitude is the Distinguishing Wisdom of Amitabha, who is in the posture of meditation, in which you recognize not only the essential equality but also the differences among living beings. By respecting them, you come to the fourth attitude, conditioned by tolerance and compassion, which finds its expression in Amoghasiddhi's gesture of blessing and reassurance, resulting in karma-free action.

All these four attitudes are combined in the center, where Vairochana is enthroned in the gesture of setting in motion the Wheel of the Dharma, the universal law. Since the Buddha Shakyamuni is also sometimes seen in this mudra, Vairochana is shown with two lions as throne-bearers.

Now, the question arises, are these Dhyani-
Buddhas less real because they are not historical? My
answer would be: They are more real, in so far as
they can be experienced in meditation. A mind-
created reality may even take outer form because
"form is not different from emptiness (shunyata), the
Plenum-Void," as has been said in the Sutra of Transcendental Wisdom *(Prajnaparamita-sutra)*. Here begins the great mystery of Reality which can only be
solved in the experience of meditation and in the creative visions of immortal art.

Part Three

TRUSTING EXPERIENCE

The Realm
of Religion

The realm of religious life is a specific form of human experience or, better, an expression of an inner experience. Therefore no objective scientific description can ever do justice to the realm of religion, since it cannot grasp what is most essential. At the very moment in which the subjective experience is treated as the object of intellectual observation or inquiry, it is robbed of its aliveness and immediacy.

Without doubt, each religion has characteristics which can be described and interpreted, but each interpretation is already an expression of our subjective point of view. This is true even more so, since we always have to translate the word symbols of a foreign language—often no longer spoken in our time and rooted in the way of thinking of a time long since gone—into the medium of our own language, the product of our contemporary culture. Such translation requires an unusual degree of sympathetic understanding, which can develop only in a person who for years has completely identified himself with the ideas of a still living religious tradition to such a degree that, in an act of creative re-appreciation, he can assimilate and integrate it.

Unfortunately, sympathetic understanding of this sort is exactly what most translators and interpreters who have been trained in scientific philology and history of culture are lacking. Often they are unable to let go of preconceived and, to some degree, generally accepted ideas. For the sake of being "scientific" in their work, they are often unwilling to open themselves to the realm of religious experience they have undertaken to interpret. But it is precisely this willingness to open ourselves to new experiences which is the indispensable prerequisite for the ability, based on our own experience instead of mere theorems, to give others at least a sense of the true essence of a religion.

 Each religion is a mirror of the psychic states of human beings who, under different social and cultural conditions, expressed their religious experiences. All value judgments, as well as the distinction between primitive and highly developed religions, do not apply here, since a so-called "savage" is often closer to transcendental experiences than many members of highly sophisticated cultures whose feelings are blocked by scores of prejudices and who are no longer capable of a wholistic understanding of life. Therefore their religious life is reduced to social patterns of behavior and forms which are separated from everyday life.

The loss of wholeness means at the same time a loss of our own center, evidenced by our tendency to split our lives up into separated spheres. This development of Western culture already concerned Goethe when he told his contemporaries, "Nature has neither kernel nor shell. It is all in one." Experience is always wholistic and does not know the exclusiveness of Aristotelian logic.

What is needed in our time, therefore, is a stimulation and rejuvenation of religious experience, while always keeping in mind that the experiences we have reflect our respective state of inner maturity. In the course of our development, our experiences change continually, and we in turn are changed by them.

This experience of constant change makes us capable of respectfully regarding other religious forms of experience, without making hasty judgments. On the contrary, we willingly make an effort to understand all forms of religious experience, without necessarily having to take them on as our own. This is the foundation for genuine tolerance, which does not waive an independent decision-making.

If we want to grasp the living essence of a religion, we always have to keep in mind that *each* religion is something alive and organic, always growing and changing and constantly reevaluating all values handed down. Whenever this process stops, the religious life freezes into dogmas, and the expression of immediate life experience becomes scholastical, degenerating, in turn, to a merely traditional form which is bare of all life.

If we realize that religions are like living organisms, we have to take into account their respective historical phases of development, since they are by necessity an expression of aliveness and growth. On the one hand, they are characterized by the development of the initial seed-like tendencies. On the other hand, they are influenced by the changing cultural and social circumstances of their surroundings.

The starting point of Buddha's teachings differs from other religions insofar as he based them on universal human experience without recourse to an already consolidated religious form. Buddha was not interested in what somebody else believed or thought might be possible, but in what he was doing in a responsible way to make life easier for himself and his fellow human beings and to strive for a higher goal. He did not attempt to reform the Vedic tradition, as has often been assumed; he was breaking away from the basic principles of the Brahmanic-Vedic faith, a religious system that was based upon rituals of sacrifice, rules for purification, and social castes, but not on the recognition of ethical values such as holiness of all forms of life *(ahimsa)* and the self-responsibility of each human being, whose dignity is not dependent on caste or color of the skin *(varna)*.

92

Therefore, the roots of early Buddhism cannot be found in the soil of the Vedic-Brahmanic tradition, but in an autochthonal, very ancient Indian tradition (as Buddha himself once remarked) which had as the basis of its religious life one's own effort *(shrama)* and ethical responsibility *(shila)*, instead of bloody sacrifices *(yajna)* and hereditary priesthood. This is the reason why Buddha was, among other epithets, rightfully called "the Great Shramana."

In the same way as his contemporary Mahavira, the reformer and rejuvenator of Jainism, Buddha rested upon a pre-Aryan tradition which remained alive during the reign of the conquerers who intruded from the northwest only as an underground movement. Ideas such as karma, dependent origination, rebirth and liberation, non-violence *(ahimsa)*, and compassion *(karuna)* were completely unknown to the Vedic way of thinking. They were only later assimilated—mainly through the influence of Buddhism—by the popular forms of Hinduism which also integrated essential concepts of Jainism.

Hinduism as we know it today is a relatively late development reaching back to the fourteenth century. The expression "Hindu" itself was used for the first time by the Arabic scholar and traveler Alberuni, who used it as a generic term for all the peoples living beyond the Sindhu (Indus) river. In later times, the social system and the wealth of religious views were lumped together as Hinduism.

Thus Hinduism as we know it today is a relatively late development of Indian religion. Therefore it is wrong to maintain that Buddhism developed out of Hinduism which, on the contrary, was in its beginning influenced by essential elements of Buddhism. But it is difficult to let go of long-standing prejudices, and even more so since previous generations, having only limited knowledge of the historical development of the religions, regarded the Vedic religion as the origin of all Indian thinking. Only the discovery of the magnificent urban cultures at the Indus, like those of Harappa and Mohenjo Daro, made us aware that there was a highly developed pre-Vedic and pre-Brahmanic culture, a fact which was still unknown to the pioneering Indologists of the last century.

Recent research work, like that of professor Lal Mani Joshi, makes it evident that there is no reason to assume a time before the sixth or fifth century B.C. for the origins of the oldest Upanishads. This understanding has also been supported by Indologists like S. N. Dasgupta, A. A. Macdonell, Max Mueller, Winternitz, Jacobi, and others. Therefore it seems unlikely that the Buddha was influenced by the teachings of the Upanishads, which were never mentioned, let alone quoted, in the Buddhist texts, as was the case with the teachings of other contemporary philosophers. It is much more likely that the Upanishads were influenced by Buddhist ideas and those pre-Vedic and non-Vedic religious traditions that were transmitted as

94

a living heritage in Jainism and in the teachings of certain circles of roaming ascetics (shramanas). Only then is it understandable why the Upanishads were regarded as secret teachings that contradicted the Vedic tradition.

Now that the philological basis of the Buddhist teachings has been to a large extent explained by the unselfish research work of generations of Indologists, it is time to gain an understanding of the psychological background of Buddhist thinking and feeling and to make it accessible to people of our times.

The Buddha neither claimed to be the bearer of a divine revelation nor of preaching an ancient religious tradition, but rested firmly on the basis of experience. As we already noted, he did not ask his followers to have blind faith, but to strive uncompromisingly and honestly for an unselfish way of life for the sake of both the individual and his fellow beings. His teachings are an invitation: "Come and see! Open your eyes to the facts of life and be honest in dealing with yourself. Do not try to escape from self-inflicted suffering, but transcend its origin, which is within yourself. What is important is not your faith or your opinions, but only what you are doing! You are the heir of your actions, thoughts, and intentions, independent of what you think is your ego or are your possessions. Open yourself to the experience of what you call the world. Being in the world, you experience in your six-feet-high physical body: It is the foundation of your

95

experience, the experience of the arising and disappearance of the world."

It was not the Buddha's intention to invent a new theory about the origin of the world and the cosmos, but to make us aware that the only cosmos which we can observe and significantly influence is our own body with its psycho-physical functioning. He realized that the functions of our body as well as those of our consciousness are not erratic, but behave according to those natural laws which we interpret according to the level of our development and understanding and then project onto inner events.

In the tantric teachings of the Vajrayana, as it developed in the course of some centuries after Buddha's Parinirvana, this idea is more strongly emphasized. It is written in the Buddhist Tantras that our body is not limited to this or that material form, but is an expression of the whole universe which, in turn, created this body with all of its organs and mental-psychic properties. In tantric meditation our realm of experience opens up to the realization of higher dimensions, in which we can participate as soon as our awareness has transcended the limitations of the realm of three-dimensional materiality.

As the Buddha himself explained even in the Pali canon, this experience of the transcendental cannot be grasped by means of logical and dialectical thinking; therefore it is also beyond the realm of verbal description. This is why in the Pali canon it is said of the Dharma, "Well proclaimed is the law *(dhamma)* by the Enlightened One: visible to everybody, timeless, deep, understandable only for the wise ones *(sanditthiko, akaliko, ehipassiko, paccatam veditabbo vinnuhi)*." The simplicity of this praise of the Dharma can only be confusing for intellectuals, but those who have acquired wisdom, who have regained their inner wholeness, will immediately understand.

However, until this inner unity and wholeness has been found again, human beings blindly follow the all-pervasive force of the impulse to live *(tanha)*. Taken by itself, this impulse is neither good nor bad, but for the individual it can turn into the one or the other as long as he or she is separated from the light of realization that we all are connected with everything. Awareness that the individual is embedded in the universal is the only immanent power which can propel us beyond the limitations of isolation.

Therefore ignorance *(avidya)* is the first link in the chain of dependent origination *(pratityasamutpada)* which the Buddha proclaimed, i.e., the ignoring of that all-connectedness in which nothing can exist in isolation and without being connected to the whole, even though we may not be aware of this fact. This not-wanting-to-see the actuality (actuality in the sense of those factors that have an influence on us, but not a realm of merely mentally produced "objective" things) has nothing to do with the ordinary usage of the term "stupidity" or a lack of intelligence, but is that background out of which the subconscious formative powers *(samskara)* grow. In the usual human consciousness (= waking mind), they lead to that differentiation which splits the world into a dualistic view of self and non-self, me and you, within and without, my possessions and your possessions: in short, into subject and object.

As a result of that splitting of the consciousness, we become aware of our mental-corporeal totality *(nama-rupa)* which, by means of the six sense realms *(sadayatana)*, makes contact *(sparsa)* with the respective sense objects, whereby feelings *(vedana)* mature into perceptions and sensations which in turn are either pleasurable or unpleasurable, or neither, or both. Unpleasant feelings motivate us to avoid everything that would make us endure them anew. Pleasurable sensations, however, lead to the desire to experience them again, so that an urge arises *(trishna*, literally "thirst")*, which prompts in us the wish to hold onto that which gives us pleasure and to make it our possession *(upadana)*. This wish to possess and to hold onto leads us again and again into the realm of becoming *(bhava)* and change, i.e., into the realm of birth *(jati)*, and therefore into the realm of old age and death *(jara-marana)*.

In the course of this constant process of becoming, there is only one point where we can interfere and give it another direction: our consciousness *(vijnana)*. Only our consciousness is not limited to the uninterrupted process of becoming aware of ourself in contrast to the world, but is also able to experience our relatedness to the world as a whole as well as our connections with all beings. Out of the awareness of our inseparable relatedness within the universe, and therefore of our essential connectedness with sentient beings, those four meditations originated which Buddha called the four immeasurables or the divine abidings: the development of an all-penetrating awareness of love, compassion, joy, and an impartial equanimity *(maitri, karuna, mudita,* and *upeksha)*. The latter is defined as the ability to disregard one's own suffering, but not to be careless about the suffering of others. *Upeksha* is that mental equilibrium *(tatramajjhattata)* which grows within the human being through love, compassion, and joy and which enables him to embrace all beings without discrimination and without boundaries, identifying with all of them.

Pratityasamupada—conditioned origination—is not to be understood as being merely a causal connection. It is the attempt to describe a linkage which is simultaneously or together arising, and which can be understood as a temporal sequence as well as a timeless simultaneous becoming. Thus, it can be interpreted as a logical sequence on the one hand, and as immediate synchronicity of complex processes on the other. The Buddha rejected neither understanding, although he preferred synchronicity and conditionality, as can be gathered from an explanation given by the Buddha himself to his disciple Ananda when the latter interpreted the formula all too hastily as easily understandable on the logical level. From the fact that the Buddha repeatedly omitted some links of the chain when explaining the "dependent origination in simultaneity," it is also evident that it is not to be understood as a rigid dogma of Buddhist thought, but merely as "a finger pointing to the moon," important only in that everything in this world behaves according to dependent origination.

Seen from this perspective, the term *akaliko,* timeless or synchronous, begins to make sense. As long as he was speaking on the level of ordinary human thinking, the Buddha always adhered to the rules of logic and dialectic. But he was aware that all that happens is by its nature timeless. At the same time he rejected any kind of metaphysics as mere thought products, and therefore any kind of speculation about the realm of the transcendental. He stripped terms like nirvana and karma of their metaphysical interpretations, so that nirvana is not that quietistic ideal of "dissolving" in the cosmos, but is defined by the Buddha in a purely psychological way as the cessation of greed, hatred, and ignorance. He did not say anything about the transcendental significance of the term nirvana *(anupadisesa-nibbana)* which could serve as a basis for human fantasy. The term karma in Buddhism was not described by the Buddha as an unqualified fatalism, which would turn each instant and every action into a fetter which ties us—consciously or unconsciously—to the past. In Buddhist understanding, karma means "action" in the sense of a completed intentional activity based on a conscious decision (*cetana*), which will therefore induce a similar attitude under comparable circumstances in the future.

Dwight Goddard, the editor of *The Buddhist Bible* (an anthology of Buddhist texts), describes karma as "habit energy" in his translation of the *Lankavatara Sutra*. In this sense, what we call karma manifests as the tendency to repeat similar actions like a machine unless a new motivation occurs, like a total "change in the deepest seat of our consciousness." If this were not possible, no liberation could ever happen. Therefore the Buddha called "the miracle of change," i.e., the change of intention based on honest conviction, the only miracle worth striving for.

In the same way as he discouraged the hankering after miracles by pointing out the only essential miracle, he also stripped away the metaphysical meaning of the terms ego or self (*atman*) in the sense of an eternal and unchangeable principle of monadic egohood. Instead, he realized the experience of I as a focus of individual consciousness, changing in each moment, the necessary precondition for any balanced experience of the inner and outer as well as for each reasonable action. However, if this so-called I is elevated to an independently and automatically functioning principle of unrestrained self-centeredness, it develops into a factor which propels the individual toward destruction, similar to cancer which, by its unrestrained growth, destroys the very organism which should be preserved and maintained.

Although Buddhist psychology does away with everything which resembles the Western understanding of a "soul monad" in the ordinary sense, from the very beginning it paid special attention to those mental processes which we collectively call "the psyche," since these are the dynamic forces which characterize human beings and open them to the path to liberation and enlightenment.

Therefore, the Buddhist teachings of no-self *(anatman)* are not teachings about "no-soul" or "noessence:" they mean a breaking open and tearing down of the self-established walls by which human beings separate, encapsulate, and close themselves off from all other beings so that they, in their inability to transcend the boundaries of egocentricity, are incapable of love, being sympathetic with others, and rejoicing in others' happiness. And since they do not fully realize these three mental powers to a degree of unlimited impartiality, they will also never accomplish that inner balance which is the prerequisite of the great liberation.

We are living in a time of linguistic inflation in which words increasingly lose their inner significance and meaning, or just become shallow. Words used to be—in the West, too—an expression of an idea (Greek: *eidos*), i.e., of something envisioned, but they have suffered degeneration to a "terminus" i.e., to something limited and clearly defined, which mummifies the previously living and changeable significance of the vision. Nowadays we are witnessing a further depletion of the meaning of language, which makes the living transmission of the Dharma through the written word even more difficult, although in the West illiteracy is almost completely abolished.

Translators of ancient languages are often not aware that, because meaning shifted in the course of the millenia, even a literal translation gives the modern reader incorrect ideas, since the modern reader is used to thinking in abstract terms and is no longer rooted in the pictorially evocative language of ancient times. Those translators also lead the reader astray who, in an interpretative fashion, impute the language of modern psychology, psychotherapy, and philosophy to a time when understanding and comprehension were much more direct and unmediated, with access to the mythical and magical mode of thinking. The language of ancient times was therefore much more differentiated in the realm of emotions than our present colloquial language.

In this connection I have repeatedly pointed out that the usual translation of the Buddhist word *maitri* as "friendship," "benevolence," "kindness" etc. is a warping and deflation of its meaning. The word *maitri* is certainly connected with the Sanskrit word *mitra*, which means "friend." But what did a friend mean for the people of the Buddha's time? A friend was the closest confidant from whom nothing was expected (although one was willing to give him everything) and to whom one was completely attentive without any limitations, up to the point of being ready to lose even one's own life in his service. How easily do we in our time call every passing acquaintance a "friend," although his inner being is as alien to us as the sun of a remote galaxy.

The above-mentioned translations for *maitri*, which simply means "love," were probably chosen because in the puritanical Victorian age translators were anxious to avoid all possible sexual connotations of the word "love." Therefore they bent over backwards instead of understanding that "love" is a matter of the heart on the various levels of being human. Love grows to the extent of our own inner growth, transcending all rationality and any coldly calculating mental attitude by embracing another human being in a stance of open sympathy.

Thus, translating *maitri* with the words "friendship" and "benevolence," in their modern meaning, robs it of its original depth of meaning and implies an ethically sterile and colorless attitude toward our fellow beings. The Buddha clearly defined *maitri* with these words, "Just as a mother protects her son, her only child, with her own life, so will I develop a boundlessly open heart for all sentient beings."

The Pali word *ceta*, which was here rendered as "heart," can also be translated as "mind" or—as Neumann translated quite correctly—as "Gemut."[1] On other occasions I have repeatedly pointed out the often inadequate translation and interpretation of Buddha's three basic teachings (Pali *tilakkhana*). I do not want to dwell on it in detail, only to clarify once again that *sabbe sankhara* does not mean—as Neumann rendered it—"the whole being," but the realm of subconscious impulses which, as long as we hold onto the erroneous concept of ego, will by necessity lead to an experience of suffering.

The negation of the ego-experience in the third of the three basic teachings, *sabbe dhamma anatta*, does not refer to "the whole world," as Neumann says, but simply points out the fact that all *dhammas*, i.e., "all elements of reality" (and this means both those which create in our consciousness the multitude of forms as well as the uncreated *dhamma nibbana*), are without ego. No-ego, however, does not mean "no-being," as it was interpreted by Neumann and other philologists.

How untrustworthy are the philologically correct, and on the level of their content how different translations often are, is evident in the interpretative rendering of words which are of significant importance for an understanding of Buddhism, such as shunyata,

105

siddha, and siddhi. The philological equivalent in our language for shunyata is "emptiness, voidness." This, however, is not identical with "nothingness" or "nothing," as they are often explained. In Buddhism, the concept "nothingness" can be used for the most part with regard to the seventh stage of meditative absorption (Pali *jhana*), the "realm of nothingness" *(akincannayatana)*. This is because emptiness is always the emptiness *of* something. With regard to the question, "Empty of what?," early Buddhism always answered, "empty of an ego and all propositions." Put in a positive way, as was done by the Mahayana, the answer should be, "free of all limitations and restrictions," and thus of unlimited potentiality.

It was this interpretation which gave Nagarjuna's philosophy as well as the whole of Mahayana such an impetus and saved it from a merely rational understanding of the Buddha Dharma. If we perceive shunyata from that perspective, we can understand the enthusiasm with which his idea was received by the religious circles of Asia.

Another translation which led to similar erroneous views was rendering the term siddha (completely realized ones, perfected ones) as "sorcerer." The siddhas belonged to a group of medieval mystics, living in the sixth to the tenth centuries, who rejected all forms of orthodoxy and influenced the whole of religious life in India. Both Buddhists and Hindus claim the eighty-four great siddhas for themselves.

Poets and philosophers from all walks of life and all social classes, the siddhas did not recognize either castes or any distinctions of status and spoke the respective colloquial language instead of the scholarly Sanskrit. Tibetan descriptions, in particular, preserved their life stories.

The biographies of the siddhas were translated into German at the beginning of this century by a specialist under the unfortunate title "The 84 Sorcerers" *(Die 84 Zauberer)*. Since the author was obviously unable to grasp the essential message of that unorthodox, provocative form of Buddhist mystical methodology, the book completely missed the main point. Furthermore, since it was written in rather dry language, hardly anybody read it. How absurd it is to translate siddha as "sorcerer" is already evident in the fact that Buddha's worldly name was Siddhartha, i.e., the one who has realized or reached the goal *(artha)*. Just because according to popular legends the siddhas performed miracles is no reason to call them "sorcerers," just as no one would call Jesus a sorcerer because he is said to have performed miracles.

Other erroneous interpretations of Buddhist concepts occur if the terms used are already colored by certain popular ideas. This is especially true in the case of the Buddhist teachings on rebirth. Rebirth is often thought of as the migration of a soul, in the sense of a soul monad migrating from body to body. As understood by Buddhists, this incident would better be called a "transformation of the soul" than a "migration of the soul." When King Menander asked the wise Nagasena whether the one who has been reborn is the same as the one who died in his previous life, the answer was, "Na ca so, na ca anno. Neither the same one nor another one!" This is because "We do not jump into the same river twice" (Heraclitus). This is not only because the river is changing from moment to moment, but also because we ourselves are never exactly the same from one moment to the next.

We become aware of our development and growth, which is happening at each moment, only when we review more extensive periods of time. Then we realize that this child became a teenager, turned into an adult, and eventually reached old age. And this is when we become aware that in each human being there are "many human beings," simultaneously present. The so-called identity is one of those abstractions of Aristotelian logic which is, like all other statistical averages, a simplification without which scientific work would be almost impossible. However, are there in real life identical trees, animals, or human beings? There are certainly similarities in life, but never identities. Therefore, the relationship between childhood and old age is not based on the identity of the person, but on the conditioned origination of constantly changing existential conditions which develop according to the direction we chose to go (or according to karmic tendencies).

Human beings may strive for "being," but precisely because we are striving for it, we always remain
in the process of becoming and are able to rise above
the process of becoming only in the act of transcending
to the great liberation. However, being a human being
means to be in the process of becoming; this is why
the Buddha emphasized the process of becoming as
the law which governs all forms of life, and why
Buddhist psychology talks about the *bhavanga-sota*, the
"stream of becoming." It is this stream of becoming,
however, which we experience again and again as the
reason for our suffering, because of our attachments
and our holding on. But the Buddha's main intention
was to end suffering, and therefore it is natural that
the Four Noble Truths culminate in the "Eightfold Path
which leads to the cessation of suffering."

Here the question arises: Is this Eightfold Path
(*astangikamarga*) a path in distinct steps, leading step
by step toward the goal, or is it a path which as a whole
has eight links, but has to be increasingly realized in
its totality?

Most interpreters prefer the idea of a gradual path
in steps. Consequently, they practice the individual
links or steps and have, relatively soon, certain results
which give both teacher and student a preliminary
feeling of security. However, these results all remain
in a realm which has but little resemblance to the lofty
goal. The reason is that even the first step on this path
(*samyak-drishti*) has to embrace the highest level of

insight *(samyak-samadhi)* in order to be able to make the decisive decision *(samyak-samkalpa)*, referring to the total human being, as a result of which everything else follows by necessity.

Here, too, the erroneous and shallow translation of a word, namely *samyak* (Skt.), or *samma* (Pali), or *yang-dag* (Tib.), as "right, correct," implying a relative evaluation, leads into a certain direction of thought oriented toward value statements. However—as I have been pointing out for decades—*samyak* has a much deeper and broader meaning. It is an expression of wholeness, or of the balance between action and mental attitude, in which the total human being participates, so that it expresses itself in his way of thinking, speaking, and acting as a living, dynamic totality at rest in his own inner center—just like that personage we behold in the image of the Buddha: the *samyak-sambuddha*, the completely enlightened one. The Tibetan equivalent for the Sanskrit term *samyak*, namely *yang-dag*, inspires us to an even deeper understanding, since this word includes the sense of being totally in accord with the middle path taught by the Exalted One: all-embracing and harmonizing, free of all extremes.

It is exactly this inner attitude which Buddha made the basis of his teachings: *samyak-samadhi* (the last link of the Eightfold Path) designates total integration, becoming whole and one. As long as we have not realized this wholeness, we have to strive continuously for the total integration of all our psychic factors, and we have to do so in going through the Eighfold Path repeatedly on increasingly higher levels of experience, as on a spiral. However, on whichever level we realize the circle of eight links, the basis of our effort is marked by *samyak*, i.e., by the unconditioned and unlimited engagement of the totality of our mental and spiritual properties and powers. Such an engagement of our energetic potential *(virya)* transcends by far all merely moralistic or intellectual motives. It is not an expression of a mere momentary enthusiasm, but the result of key experiences which cause a change on the deepest levels of the personality and lead to such a compelling urge in the direction of the lofty goal that all one-sidedness in our way of thinking, speaking, feeling, and acting is excluded.

Samyak-drshti becomes therefore the basic attitude of the Buddhist practitioner. It is an attitude of total, unbiased openness which enables us to perceive a situation as it is *(yatha-bhutam)*, i.e., to look at events and situations not just from one side (and, above all, not from a frozen ego-stance which we stubbornly maintain); but to strive constantly without prejudices (and without excluding what we personally feel is uncomfortable) to look from all possible angles at the object of our investigation. Therefore we will not repress and close our eyes before anything that is painful, which hurts our vanity, or which makes us feel aggressive, but we will become aware of the conditions and causes at their basis. And when we realize

111

that our reactions to conditions and causes arises from within ourselves, we will do everything we can to transcend them.

> ". . . to accept that which is given, which is imposed on us, not to avoid it externally, but to follow it to the deeper levels, no longer to resist the pressure of conditions, but to use it in order to apply it on a deeper, denser, more uniquely ours, level of our own being."[2]   —Rilke

However, if we use the redirection of the pressure into our own being, into the deeper levels of our own consciousness, in such a way that we numb ourselves against our environment and the suffering in the world, even to the point of being careless, and then call it "inner letting go" and "nonattachment," then we deny Buddha's main concern, namely the unlimited development of *maitri*, *karuna*, and *mudita*, the unlimited warm and selfless love and sympathy for others' fate. Only through this development can arise what the Exalted One called *ceto-vimutti*, the liberation of heart and mind.

Notes

1. Gemut: There is no exact English equivalent for the German word Gemut, which connotes both a feeling mind and a warm heart.

2. Rilke, *Letter from Muzot*, p. 130.

Meditation in the Vajrayana: First Steps

The emergence of Buddhism, whose roots can be traced back to the pre-Aryan period of Indian culture, marked the beginning of a new developmental stage of human-cultural existence on the Indian subcontinent. Earlier there was, as in other parts of the world, a magical era, which was followed by the era of the gods or myths. The era starting with Buddhism I would like to call "the era of reason." However, I do not want "reason" to be understood in the same sense as this term is used in the United States and Europe at the present time.

In India "reason" was then considered to be only the foundation upon which the higher intuitive understanding was based. Thus Buddha said that his teachings are profound and hard to understand by the average mind since they transcend discursive thinking. He took for granted the existence of a reality which could be explained and demonstrated by rational means, but without being bound solely by mental or logical considerations. He knew that what he wanted to point at transcended the realm of rationality and was accessible only through experience.

Buddha Shakyamuni therefore maintained that experience deserves the highest rank. Thus he told the Kalamers, "Do not go by hearsay, not by traditions, not by the opinion of the day, not by the authority of holy scriptures, not by mere reasoning or logical conclusions, not by theoretical considerations or preferred opinions, not by your impression of personal values, not by the authority of a master. But if you yourself understand, based on your own experience, that these things are wholesome, leading toward well-being and benefit, then you should strive for it." (*Anguttara Nikaya III*, 66) In other words, it is not the belief in something that is most important; experience is what is crucial.

Under certain circumstances belief can certainly lead to an initial opening. For example, a certain degree of trust in a teacher is a prerequisite to benefitting from his teachings. But after one has listened to a teaching one has to decide whether it is consistent with one's own experience. Only then should one try to apply it in one's own life. If it proves practical one should embrace it. Never should blind confidence or mere belief be the basis for adhering to teachings, for a charismatic or suggestive person could then easily drag others into religious or ideological paranoic notions.

114

Often I have been asked why the Buddha never said anything about gurus. He never said anything against them, but he knew that most people will follow a teacher blindly because they think he is a guru or priest and therefore he must know what is good for them. However, the Buddha rejected such disowning of one's discriminative faculties. Only that which does not contradict reason and which is sensible can be a basis for the Buddhadharma; what contradicts reason and is not sensible is certainly not part of Buddhism.

One could of course ask why Buddhists use mantras, mandalas, and mudras, which to a large extent are beyond the grasp of reason and not part of our immediate experience. The answer is that one can certainly use mantras, mandalas, mudras and other helpful means as long as one knows what one is doing. It would be totally senseless to accept and do something only because it seems to be "nice." So much of what seems to be "nice" may not be true and in accordance with reality. At first glance it may be very convincing, but later it will not hold up to experience.

Nowadays many people are of the opinion that chanting mantras presupposes a belief in mantras. Well, one has to have *confidence,* but confidence by itself is not sufficient, because having confidence in a mantra should be based on knowing what one is saying. If one does not understand what one is chanting, the whole process is pure self-deception. Perhaps it may sometimes help like a pain-killer which one takes when one is in pain or difficulties in order to suppress or to forget them for a moment. But this is no reason for using a mantra.

For example, let's look at Guru Padmasambhava's mantra: OM AH HUM VAJRA GURU PADMA SIDDHI HUM. The meaning of this mantra is profound. If, for instance, one chants OM AH HUM, then this makes sense only if it is used in conscious connection with certain internal centers. Thus OM refers to the *sahasrara* chakra (crown center), AH to the throat chakra, and HUM to the heart center. One should not take this too literally because the chakras mentioned in Buddhist psychology are not at all identical with the physical organs: neither with the brain, the throat, or the heart, nor with the nerve centers located in their vicinity. Such an identification was never intended.

The idea behind this simile in Buddhism is that we associate certain qualities of consciousness with certain parts of the body. For example, if one says "I" then one points automatically toward the center of one's chest. And why? One does not point exactly toward one's heart, but to the place where one senses one's own center. This explains why in India and Asia, including Tibet, Japan, and China, the "heart" is seen as being identical with our deepest psychic movements, our deepest thoughts, and our deepest intuition. This means that intuition does not depend on our brain but on our "heart." In previous centuries "heart" was associated with feeling and sensing, and the brain with

116

thinking and intelligence. It is in accord with reality that the brain manifests itself mainly in intellectual thinking activity, but mere intellectual thinking is not what is needed in Buddhism. More is required. This is why we speak of *prajna* and *upaya*. *Prajna* means understanding based on wisdom, and *upaya* refers to activity based on love and compassion. If one develops wisdom without love then the wisdom will be cold and dead, leading nowhere; likewise, compassion without wisdom will end in an emotional swamp, without the means to help either oneself or others.

If we want to understand Buddhist mantras, we first have to associate them with certain centers of consciousness within our own body. We have to understand that we do not have only a head center, a throat center, and a heart center, but also centers which are associated with the "elements" earth, water, fire, etc. All those centers which we create in a process of becoming conscious have special functions based upon their symbolic position within the body. Unfortunately, modern psychology has not yet become aware of that possibility.

What is needed in our time is to "awaken" the various centers within the human body in order to become complete human beings, because we have not yet become whole. And because we are not yet whole, we are knowledgeable only in the realms of technology and thinking. Thereby we became so abstract in our imaginations that we chase nothing but shadows, for an abstract concept can mean everything or nothing at all. It can be filled with all kinds of interpretations without being backed up by any real experience.

If, however, somebody has had a real inner experience, then he will try to express it. As long as one has not experienced a mantra deep within oneself and "knows" what it means—with what it is connected, what its background is—it is nothing but empty sound, without meaning and therefore also devoid of any effect.

Unfortunately, many people believe that mantras have some kind of magical power. But as I already said, the era of magic is long gone and we are now living in a completely different era, namely the era of "Man." In the Indian era of magic one did not see any difference between oneself and somebody else, between subject and object. At that time the whole world seemed to be animated and it was possible to have unmediated contact with all things and to perceive oneself as part of the whole. This, no doubt, was wonderful. But then, in the course of time, human beings developed a certain self-awareness and we began to perceive ourselves as separate beings, separate from the world around. This was the era when the first abstract ideas were created. Thus deities were perceived as various forces existing outside human beings and capable of influencing our life. Therefore it was necessary to honor the deities and give them prayers and offerings.

The Buddha was probably the one who inaugurated the era of Man, i.e., our era. He was interested neither in worlds above nor in worlds below nor in this or that form of being. He was interested in only one thing: the human consciousness. And therefore he declared that human beings can be liberated only by means of their own efforts. But in order to do that, we first have to know who we are and what we are. Furthermore, we need to understand that this environment is conditioned and that to a great extent we are conditioned by how we interpret it, i.e., how we see it, feel it, and perceive it. We also have to understand that we are part of this universal conditioning so that we cannot separate ourselves from it and will again and again be forced to accommodate to it.

All of this makes clear that Buddha did not base his religion on abstract principles. He did not preach an all-powerful creator god or an "eternal soul," but only asked, "What did you experience? What are you doing?" And he explained, "Your actions have to be in the right relationship to your inner knowledge and to what you already understand." With that he gave his Dharma a strictly rational basis, although he by no means believed that logic could really liberate human beings. But he again and again emphasized its value for the first steps on the path. Nowadays it is fashionable in certain Buddhist circles to condemn the intellect right away. But before one can leave the intellect behind—in a certain sense at the side—one first has to

119

develop it fully. People who today throw away their intellect before they have developed it chase after this or that guru in the belief that he can liberate them. But it has to be very clearly said: Nobody but we ourselves can liberate ourselves, not even a Buddha or Bodhisattva. They are guides, and through their guidance they are helpers on our way.

On the other hand, meeting a real guru does not have to be without great value: It can help us to shorten the way and avoid detours. But even a guru is only a good helper and guide: We have to do the work ourselves. If we do not want or can not do this, then nobody can do it for us.

In Padmasambhava's mantra, we start with OM AH HUM. Here we already meet an essential and important feature of Buddhism. OM is the sound symbol of the universal. A is the sound of the human language (in the Indian alphabet the consonants can only be pronounced together with a short A following the sound of the letter). A is also the first sound that a newly born child utters. A is always the first sound, because it is the one which is the easiest to pronounce. HUM, on the other hand, is the opposite pole to the OM. It represents the depth of the human heart—of our own inner experience.

Today it is easy to speak about universal laws and the facts of the universe. But if we do not really have control over the material realm, "everything" is nothing but a beautiful but empty idea. If one wants to talk about the universal, then one should first have understood the universal *within oneself.* But this can only be realized if we have first experienced ourselves as individual beings. Thus one could say that OM as the sound of the universal is the highest goal. AH represents the level of culture, so to speak: the level of speech, thoughts, and ideas. HUM reveals the depth of our feelings and emotions.

After OM AH HUM follow the words VAJRA GURU. They refer to Padmasambhava, who is here invoked in this way because he leads to an understanding of the unchangeable and indestructible vajra, the symbol of emptiness. The Sanskrit word "Padma," which means lotus flower, is in the Tibetan language pronounced "peme," which is in a way incorrect. This is because in the Tibetan language the combination of the letters "dm" forms a new sound. As long as the Tibetans know what this word means, this is all right and does not make any difference, provided one does not adhere to the magical belief that the right pronunciation is crucial for the power of a mantra. If this were true, Sanskrit mantras would do poorly in Tibet, China, and Japan. Only the knowledge of their essence is important. Those who senselessly babble mantras and believe blindly in their power follow a magical belief, not a Buddhist understanding.

The PADMA, the lotus flower, here focuses our consciousness on the lotus of our heart in which all SID-

DHI—all powers of full realization—can be developed to liberate us. The SIDDHI of the heart are love and compassion. Therefore, when we speak of PADMA SID-DHI, we have always to keep in mind that this means the unfoldment of our heart in the sense that this "organ" is not only the "symbol" and "seat" of our thoughts and ideas, but also of our feelings and our intuition, because without intuition our thoughts are lifeless. Having intuitions means that something is added to mere thinking which greatly transcends it, since—as I already said—we can use logic only up to a certain point.

Although we use language for communication, we nevertheless cannot express everything unless we go beyond the rules of oral expression, which are subject to a specific methodology of thinking. Only if we have understood this will we no longer be fettered by linguistic forms. Many metaphysical systems make the great error of holding on to linguistic concepts and ideas in the belief that they can thereby grasp "reality."

How limited our expression is, and how limited therefore all linguistic concepts, ideas, and terms is shown by the following example. We say, "It is raining." But in reality the linguistic expression "It is raining" does not say anything because in this case the "it" does not refer to any real subject, but points only to the fact of "raining." Buddha was against all metaphysical speculations and conceptualizations. He emphasized that whatever a human being knows should have an equivalent either in nature or within ourselves. He rejected mere word games and playing with concepts. For example, let's take the word "nirvana." In Western understanding, this word is used by Hindus, Jains, and Buddhists in the same sense. But actually this word has a different meaning for each of the three great religions. For example, if a Hindu speaks of "nirvana," he is referring to something metaphysical. But if a Buddhist speaks about "nirvana," he is thinking about something psychological. The difference is evident. The metaphysical is based upon a theology which is different from general human psychology, because psychology encompasses everybody who possesses a human consciousness. Theology with its metaphysical basis is only valid for those who adhere to a certain system of faith.

Right from the beginning Buddha did not want to create a system, but to show a path. In doing this he started with the fact that, first of all, a human being has to touch the earth with both feet, and that we can walk only when we have firm ground under our feet. This is symbolically expressed in the earth-touching gesture, in which Buddha Shakyamuni is often depicted, with his left hand resting in his lap and his right hand touching the earth.

Already in the Pali canon Buddhas of the past are mentioned who—according to the spirit of their era—taught the people of their time an inexpressible truth through the specific development of certain characteristics. With the onset of the Mahayana the number of these enlightened beings increased infinitely. They are always depicted in different "non-natural" colors, while Buddha Shakyamuni himself certainly had a typical north Indian complexion.

Why these strange colors of the so-called Dhyani-Buddhas, i.e., enlightened beings generated and seen in meditation? The colors depicted do not correspond to naturalistic thinking, but can only be explained through the symbolism of the mandala. If we understand it then we know that a yellow Buddha has to be associated with the southern position of the mandala, a white Buddha is connected with either the center or the eastern direction, a green Buddha is located in the north, and a red Buddha rules over the west. In other words, the colors of the images refer to the position they have in the mandala. But why do we use these different colors? In a thanka, all images have a symbolic meaning and each color teaches us a deeper understanding which is derived from our immediate human experience.

If we look at the clear deep blue sky we experience more than the natural color blue: Behind it we sense the depth of space in its unending openness and emptiness, which we meet again in the unlimited depth of our own consciousness. In the Vajrayana the color "blue" stands for ether and for "shunyata," the great emptiness, which is neither a "nothing" nor a "nothingness," as some people believe in the West and in the Far East. It is, on the contrary, the "fullness of emptiness" out of which everything develops and emerges—it is the "dependent origination," the "nothingness and nonsubstantiality" of all that has come into existence. Thus behind the word-symbol "shunyata" we can find one of the key elements of the Buddhist path to liberation. Emptiness—symbolized through blue—one can find everywhere in thankas, in the water as well as in the mountains, sometimes even in lamps and in fire. But above all that one can find the blue of the sky and in this blue there appear white clouds on which are depicted various beings.

What does this mean? What we are here encountering are those five elements which are also found in our own bodies, out of which our corporality is composed. All of them have the essence of emptiness—without self-being, without ego. These elements correspond to the five Dhyani-Buddhas and their entourage of Dhyani-Bodhisattvas in the mandala, which is not—as many people believe nowadays—a mere arbitrary drawing in a geometric shape to please the eye of the perceiver, the embellishment of which is dependent on the fantasy of the artist. A mandala—literally "a circle"—is on the contrary, as understood in the Indian meditative experience (and, above all, in the understanding of the Buddhist Vajrayana), a very precise map of our own mind and consciousness. Thus it serves as a description of the path which is intended to serve our psychic development. It shows how we have to meditate, how we have to move in our own consciousness in order to arrive at the lofty goal.

Lately I have seen various mandalas made by artists or by patients of psychiatrists which looked quite nice. Of course you can call anything which is round and concentric a mandala. But this does not correspond to the meaning that word has in Sanskrit—even if eminent psychologists and psychotherapists designate these works as mandalas. A mandala is created, and has to be created, according to definite rules, rules developed thousands of years ago based on meditative experience. Therefore one cannot produce a mandala based on our own fantasy or ideas; in order to benefit human beings it has to follow those rules and laws according to which all mandalas are shaped. What are these rules?

In the center of the mandala one will always find a lotus flower with four petals which are arranged around the central calayx according to the four directions. This calayx is the holy center of the whole mandala in which all imagined lines meet. Around the holy central flower one can see the blueline drawing of a four-cornered temple with four gates. Why four gates? Because it is open to all the directions of space. The blueline of the temple is surrounded by a circle of lotus flowers or lotus petals which in the outward direction is followed by a circle of golden vajras and finally by a circle of flames. The symbolic meaning of these "protective circles" is that the temple, which is open to all sides, has to be protected from external influences. This is why there are "three walls" by which it is surrounded.

What does that mean for the practitioner? It tells him that before he starts to meditate, he has to create around himself a wall of these different elements, because during meditation one opens oneself and is therefore vulnerable to all kinds of external influences. To put it differently: During meditation one is in a receptive state of mind in which one could possibly be influenced by things to which one does not want to expose oneself. Thus the protective circle of lotus petals means the *purity of heart* which is free from all wish to possess, free from all ambitions and all envy as well as even the most subtle hate. If we are penetrated by these emotions, no meditation is possible because they "contaminate" us.

The vajra circle is a symbol of our mind which is stable and directed through accumulated energy and purposefulness and therefore unassailable. The circle of flames symbolizes the fire of wisdom in which all dualistic thinking is burned away and in the light of which we can see everything according to reality.

These symbols make it evident that meditation presupposes a change in our inner attitude: purity, clear directedness, and growing wisdom. Without these three, meditation would lead to various kinds of fantasies and purely emotional states which soon abate without truly transforming experience and which leave us disappointed.

Nowadays it has become a custom to hang mandalas up on a wall. Since maps have accustomed us to thinking that up is north and down is south, this is the—sometimes unconscious—understanding in approaching a mandala. But this is already the first grave error in looking at a mandala, because traditionally mandalas have been sand paintings, made of leveled ground, with the practitioner sitting in front of them. In the same way as the sun rises in the east and thus begins the day, the practitioner enters the mandala through the eastern gate, the door in front of which he sits. If the picture is hanging on the wall, this door corresponds to the bottom pole. The successive meditation can be compared to walking from the breaking dawn of the early morning to the light of fully developed wisdom. In this sense the practitioner circles the holy center like the sun circles the earth, until he can penetrate to the center in which all duality is dissolved.

As long as this is not understood, a mandala does not make any sense to the spectator. For him it remains nothing but a drawing, no matter what secrets he may think he can perceive in there. He looks at it like a person who is suddenly confronted with a map, but who does not know anything about the rules and laws according to which the directions have been laid out, and who does not know that blue on the map stands for water, brown means mountain ranges and green designates plains. Even on a map one can see what one will meet on the way to the goal only if one understands how the clearly and unmistakably defined directions and color symbols work.

The same is true for the mandala. Here the colors stand not only for the respective position and a certain location within the mandala, but also for the time sequence, which is always the same. And this is exactly why it is impossible to enter the mandala at just any place. It has to be entered always through the same "gate," after which one circumambulates the center in a clockwise direction.

The eastern position in most mandalas is characterized by a white color, although in some mandalas by a deep blue. Apparently blue and white are interchangeable; why this is so, I will explain later. The south is characterized by yellow, the west by red, and the north by green. Why have these colors been chosen for the corresponding directions? Where do we look for the origin?

Usually one starts meditating in the early morning, before sunrise. There is still little light and the east is either dark blue or already a little bit white. Noon is different: It is characterized by the southern direction, when the sun has reached its highest point and its golden yellow light pours evenly over everything. At the time of sunset in the west the sky turns red. This is why red becomes the color of this direction. As far as the color of the night is concerned, this is something very strange, connected with the very ancient belief that the sun renews itself at midnight. Like the sun, the human being embarks at night on the great death sojourn into the darkness of the unconscious. But while we are asleep, our life continues, our vital energies are even renewed, and this happens in a stage where our consciousness is at times not working at all, and sometimes only partially. For the people at the beginning of human history this was the proof that we can live without our consciousness.

With the breath it is very different: This process continues even without our awareness. If breath stopped, life would come to an end. This is why it was assumed very early on that it is meditation on the breath which, of all meditation techniques, can lead us immediately into the depth. And meditation on the breath is open to everyone, because we are all breathing, and we all have the ability to become fully aware of this function and thus to experience the breath in its fullness. Most of the time, however, we do not take advantage of this possibility. This is why Buddha Shakyamuni put awareness of the breath at the beginning of all meditation: It is the prerequisite. Only if we have learned to consciously experience our breath will we be capable of understanding the inner structure of this world in which we live—namely as conditioned dependent origination.

With our breath we incorporate something which exists "outside" our corporal being, and after a short while we give it back to this external realm. Thus in this existence we cannot take or acquire anything which we do not eventually have to give back. If we take in nutrients and do not dispose of them after digestion, these nutrients will turn into poison which may kill us. If we inhale air but do not exhale, we will suffocate. Whatever we take into our body, we cannot hold on to forever: At the very last moment, the moment of death, it returns to its origin. Thus in the experience of the breath we become fully aware of that law which Buddhism regards as basic, the law that life means never-ending change expressed in a continuous give and take. There is nothing we can look upon as our possession and hold on to, neither our social position nor our wealth. At the very moment in which we merely try to hold on to something, it turns into a deadly "poison."

This is also true for our worldly "possessions," which turn into a life-threatening poison if we cling to them and try to hold on to that which slips out of our control. Then we fixate and freeze, no longer able to perceive the fullness of life. But at that very moment in which we are capable of letting go of everything without clinging, we are free. Freedom does not mean that one can do whatever one wants or wishes; to be free, that is to make oneself independent of everything in the world by discovering one's own center.

131

In meditation we are trying to discover this inner centeredness, which is symbolically expressed in the so-called yoga attitude. "Attitude" is always something at the same time external and internal. The meditation attitude is therefore related to applied psychology. For example, if we sit on a chair with both feet touching the floor, we are not centered. The body needs something to prop the back against and we get stiff because we are not resting in ourselves. But if we sit cross-legged in the half or full lotus attitude, then one is right in the center of a triangle formed by the legs, and the body can rest in itself without any support for the back. If the body is centered then the mind will soon be centered, too: It is impossible to center the mind without having first centered the body!

These are the basic teachings which the Buddha expounded in the *Satipatthana-sutta*. *Satipatthana* was originally by no means that kind of analytic meditation it was made later on, but was basically a pure experience of reality and in its form of *anapanasati* a pure experiencing of the breath: When we inhale, the whole world breathes through our being. We feel that we are again filled with life. We not only feel the breath in our lungs: We can sense the living breath all the way down into our toes and the tips of our fingers. The whole body is rejuvenated by the breath—that is, if we exhale again.

Here it becomes obvious that in Buddhism, shunyata, the "emptiness," has nothing to do with

132

negation and nothingness, but is of importance for the
insight that life means change, and that we kill ourselves by becoming petrified if we resist the change of
life. But if we have confidence in change, all change
will become a rejuvenation. What we usually perceive
as "impermanence" is not only a process of disintegration, for nothing gets destroyed without something
else taking its place, emerging out of what came before
in conditioned dependence. Life is growth, and where
there is no growth there is also no life.

Aware of the importance of change and the impermanence of all that has come into being, let's turn
to that other great idea in the Buddha's teachings, that
of *anatman* or "non-self." This teaching of "non-self"
or "no ego" did not develop in mere opposition to
the teaching of the early Upanishads on the *atman*.
Buddha just made it clear that the less one thinks about
being an individual separate and distinct from others,
the more one will feel with and for others and thereby
grow beyond oneself. The more one gives the more
one receives.

We can observe this especially in regard to bodily
functions: A muscle which is used will grow stronger
instead of becoming weaker. In the same way, the
capacity of our memory will expand in relation to the
results we demand of it.

The idea of the self or the *atman* is in its roots related
to the German word "Atem" (breath). The early Upa-

nishads defined that which they called "atman" as the eleventh *prana* or breath. Therefore they understood *atman* as a dynamic function, not as something which we can hold on to, let alone possess. In the Buddha's time, however, the term *atman* had already become so petrified that it was misunderstood as being something substantial or as a "kernel" with which we can identify ourselves. Thus the word *atman*—originally a symbol for the uninterrupted dynamic change of our human existence—was robbed of its breadth and freedom by becoming equivalent to an ego essence understood as being static.

The Buddha declared that this term *atman* was invalid since it did not correspond to reality. And therefore he set in opposition to the idea of a self, which creates boundaries and separations, the teachings of the "no self" which lets us perceive the world as it really is and opens up the unlimited nature of inner and outer space. If one has had this experience of infinite space, one will no longer be afraid to lose that which one has never possessed.

Those who talk about a "self" or *atman* as a metaphysical concept or who elevate it to the idea of something "eternal" or "lasting" speak about something they have never experienced themselves and so they cannot prove its correspondence with reality. The Buddha Shakyamuni, who always made clear statements, therefore held that one should meditate as if there is no ego. In doing so, one can realize that

134

all functions of body and mind are in reality not dependent on something called "self," but on something universal which is expressed in origination in dependence.

The experience of this universal is best reached by the conscious and clear awareness of the coming and going of our breath. We breathe in an element outside of ourselves, which suddenly becomes seemingly our "own" without our being able to keep it, and which finally—slipping out of our control—becomes universal. In this way, every function of our psycho-physical organism is seen and understood as a universal function which manifests itself for one moment in our individuality. But this individuality is nothing which, separated from the rest of the world, has its own being for itself and in itself.

Only if we know that we are embedded as a part in the whole can we talk about ourselves and other beings as individuals—i.e., as unique manifestations of the universal. Once this has been experienced, our feelings will broaden from merely personal feelings to compassion for all beings.

I have tried to give you *with words* an introduction to understanding some prerequisites for Vajrayana meditation. But the words you heard are not the most important thing: They are only like a finger pointing to what is beyond. One should regard language only as a medium, not as something which in itself has meaning and importance. It is an expression of the speaker's understanding or, more correctly, his consciousness. Only by opening ourselves will it be possible to reach that level of communication in which unmediated understanding is possible—the prerequisite for being a chela on the path of meditation.

The Significance of Vaisakha

The full-moon day of Vaisakha does not merely commemorate a single historical event in the life of the Buddha, but the coincidence of three spiritually inter-connected happenings which embrace the totality of the Buddha's career: his birth, his Enlightenment, and his Final Nirvana (Parinirvana). This gives the day of Vaisakha a timeless significance and raises it beyond all merely historical considerations into the light of an ever-present event of the Spirit. It is this which unites the Buddhists of all schools, traditions, and nationalities, and which makes the figure of the Buddha into a symbol of their common aim.

Therefore Vaisakha is a day of unification, a day on which all differences arising out of our particular opinions and theories are being put aside, in order to bow down in silent veneration before the symbol of the "perfect one," the Enlightened One. It is a day on which only one desire should be alive in all true Buddhists: to strive after this perfection, this transfiguring harmony and wholeness, this true state of Enlightenment.

The fact that the Buddha lived as a man among men gives us the courage to follow him. That as a man he succeeded in overcoming the man within himself gives us the certainty that we also can overcome ourselves, that we also can transcend our human limitations and liberate ourselves from the shackles of death and rebirth.

When I say that the Buddha succeeded in overcoming the man within him, I want to express that, though he was a man in the general sense of the word, he was not *only* a man, but something more, something that reaches out into the timeless and infinite, where concepts like "man" or "not-man" lose their meaning.

This "transcendental" nature is in no way in conflict with the humanness of the Buddha; on the contrary, it only shows the inherent (though undeveloped) transcendental nature of every human being— nay, of every form of life. This is forcefully expressed in the doctrine of *anatta*, "non-ego," which means that only if we rise above ("transcend") the narrow concept of egohood (in this sense the Pali word *atta* was used by the Buddha), can we realize the transcendental nature of man.

To show that the Buddha had fully realized this and could therefore no more be represented by his actual bodily appearance, his disciples refrained from depicting it, and during the first centuries Buddhist art indicated the presence of the Buddha merely by footprints and similar symbols.

When under the influence of Greek colonial art the attempt was made to create a plastic image of the Buddha in the conventional, realistic style of Greek portraiture, it resulted in the pathetic failure of Gandhara art which, though of aesthetic and historical interest, is entirely devoid of religious inspiration. The superficiality and sterility of Gandhara statuary fortunately prevented it from creating a lasting influence. It died as quickly as it had come into existence and was soon superseded by a new wave of spiritualized art, in which the symbolic value replaced the realistic tendency in the representation of the ideal form of Buddhahood.

The symbol of the wheel, which for a long time had been used to indicate the presence of the preaching Buddha, was now transformed into the living gesture of the *Dharmachakra-mudra,* as we see it in the famous Sarnath statue. What the skill of one individual artist would never have been able to do was achieved by the patient devotion of innumerable generations of inspired artists and devotees. The ideal shape of the Buddha-image evolved slowly until all accidentals of ephemeral human existence had disappeared, and only the expression of sublime peace, wisdom, concentration, harmony, loving-kindness, and compassion was retained.

When contemplating a Buddha-statue of this type, even a man who knows nothing of the Buddha's teaching would come to the conclusion, "This, indeed, is the perfect representation of a spiritualized man, who, without losing the solid ground of reality from under his feet, accepting and ennobling his corporality without clinging to it and without being dependent on it, is at peace with himself and with the world. What serenity and happiness are mirrored in his face, what equanimity and tranquility in every limb of the body, what perfect relaxation and self-control at the same time, what profound silence and harmony! A harmony that is contagious and penetrates the beholder! There is no more doubt, no more want, no restlessness, no insecurity, no chasing after external things, no dependence on anything. There is highest bliss; in one word, completeness!"

He who can create and bring to life this image before his mental eye, or still more, he who can experience it within himself, as the great masters of meditation did and still do, in wordless absorption and selfless devotion, such a one has taken the first step towards inner transformation and liberation. He has found the attitude from which the knowledge of the eternal Dharma was and ever is born.

This image of the perfected or complete man, which has crystallized out of the millenniums of meditative experience, does not represent an arbitrarily isolated moment from the career of the Buddha, but

140

the sum total, the quintessence of his spiritual activity—just as the sacred day of Vaisakha commemorates and comprises the totality of his earthly life. For, just as the figure of the Tathagata becomes a symbol, so also his life becomes symbolic, something that is valid for all times and for all human beings, something that is the expression of an inner law.

The same attitude which the followers of the Buddha observed with regard to the visible representation of the Enlightened One can be found in the treatment of the Buddha's life-story. They refrained from a realistic, matter-of-fact biography as much as from a realistic portrayal of his features and his outer appearance. What was important to them was not the material facts and their occurrence in time or chronological sequence, but the Buddha's spiritual quest, the unfolding of his inner life, the experiences that led to his enlightenment and to the formulation of his teachings. These inner experiences were subsequently concentrated into external occurrences in the description of the Buddha's life, and gave rise to the most beautiful and profoundly true symbolism of art and poetry, which carried the eternal message of the Buddha to the far corners of the world and did more for the propagation of Buddhism than the learned treatises of philosophers and scholars.

The so-called historical facts of the Buddha's life, however, were of so little importance that, up to the present day, it is impossible to ascertain the exact year of the Buddha's birth. Even the century in which he lived is a matter of controversy among the various Buddhist schools. They do not even agree with regard to the name of Siddhartha's wife, or whether Rahula was born before or after the Bodhisattva left his home.

In what they all agree, however, is that the Buddha proclaimed the eternal Dharma, preached by his spiritual predecessors in this world-cycle *(kalpa)* as well as aeons ago, and that this doctrine will be preached again by the future and last of the five Buddhas of this kalpa, namely Maitreya. While speaking about the Buddhas of the past and the future, the present Buddha compares their lives and actions to his own; in fact, it is only in this connection that we learn about the main events of his own life. The names of the Buddhas of this and the previous aeons are known to all Buddhist traditions.

In other words, more is known and said about the Buddha's spiritual lineage than about his human descent, though the fact that he came from a royal (or at least noble) family should have made it easy to record the lineage and the historical background of his forefathers. This shows clearly that his spiritual lineage, which might rightly be called his universal background, was regarded as being far more important than the historical and material one.

This universal background reveals one of the most profound ideas of Buddhism, which raises its teachings above the narrow concepts of dogmatic sectarianism, namely, the inescapable conclusion that the quality of enlightenment is inherent in the universe, or more correctly, latent in every form of consciousness, and therefore must come to maturity, according to universal law, whenever the conditions are favorable.

Thus, the human life of a Buddha must be seen in an entirely different perspective: It becomes a mere fraction of a far bigger and more important development, in which the human element is essentially the vehicle for the discovery of the universal (and, in this sense "transcendental") character of mind or consciousness, which according to the *Prajnaparamita-sutra*, is "inconceivable" in its true nature.

It is as inconceivable as the state of nirvana, which we cannot define by way of concepts, and of which we can only say what it is *not*. But we can imagine and visualize to some extent a human being in whom are embodied all the qualities which lead to the realization of this state. And since our striving needs an understandable, tangible, concrete Aim which is able to fill us with courage and certainty, there can be nothing more suitable than the figure of the Perfect Man, as embodied in the spiritual image of the Buddha, which—as I must emphasize again—is far more important than the ephemeral physical form of a historical personality. This personality, like everything else that has come into existence, belongs to the realm of death, while that which made Siddhartha a Buddha belongs to the Eternal.

143

Therefore the Parinirvana, this last and greatest mystery in the life of Buddha, can never be called death—for what can there be mortal in a Buddha? An Enlightened One, a Perfectly Liberated One, is subject neither to death nor to rebirth, for he who calls nothing his own can no more be identified with his material body, and therefore the dissolution of its constituents cannot affect him in any way, cannot change anything in his essential nature. Therefore it has been said:

> He who went home cannot be measured
> (any more by mundane standards):
> To speak of him, there are no words (in human
> language);
> Nothing is there that could be grasped by
> thought:
> Extinguished, therefore, are the paths of speech!
>
> Sutta Nipata 1076

This measurelessness of the enlightened mind, which is "inconceivable" to the senses and to our mundane logic (because only what is limited can be touched and perceived by the senses and grasped by the intellect), can be felt and sensed intuitively, and —on a higher plane—it can be visualized and experienced.

Then the Buddha will be to us more than a figure of the past; he will become a timeless, ever-present reality, in which we can take part every moment of our life.

So long as we cannot call up and realize the Buddha in our own consciousness, all our moral and philosophical concepts remain fragmentary and therefore lifeless and unreal. This is because our ideas and opinions remain only on the surface and do not penetrate to the sources of our being, the roots of our existence.

By visualizing the Buddha within our own mind as the living embodiment of the imperishable Dharma, we shall find the strength to follow his sacred path until we ourselves have reached the aim of Buddhahood. This is how the celebration of Vaisakha should inspire us and why on this day millions of devotees renew the solemn pledge to strive for enlightenment.

Deities, Helpers, and Saviors

Cosmos and chaos are the two poles of world affairs, and they are connected with each other in a conditional relationship like day and night, space and time, synchronicity and causality. A human being lives in the energy field between these two poles and participates in both, thus creating his hermaphroditic attributes as well as his suffering and his potential greatness.

Deities are the creative forces of the cosmos, but they do not have power over the chaos. They are creative in that they are capable of giving rise to harmony—but not to the world as such. Demons are those forces which lead to disintegration. But they can neither destroy human beings who follow those laws of divine harmony which are at the deepest root of their nature, nor can they create divine powers.

No deity can ever create a human being; however, human beings can, in creative actions, give form to deities as embodiments of their highest yearning and striving. This happens not by an act of volition as the product of a conscious act of creation, but as the flowering of their still slumbering innermost being which—to stay within the analogy—corresponds wholly to the nature of the plant from which it sprouts.

The inability of deities to create human beings is already evident from the fact that they are considered to be "perfect" beings: How, then, could they create something which is imperfect? Conversely, however, a plain seed may already contain flower and fruit in its highest perfection, in the same way as the roots, just emerging from the seed and finding their way deeper into the darkness of the earth, are already assimilating and gathering those creative forces which in the future will reveal both the flower radiant in its perfection and the ripe fruit. Therefore, it is possible that the yearning for perfection may emerge out of something imperfect: that yearning which is a creative power and which we refer to when we talk about the "divine-creative" within ourselves.

Thus we should not consider as being "full of the divine" just those people who believe in a God, but also all those who are striving to transcend themselves, whether they may believe in or deny the existence of God. Let's remember that, in our time, probably nobody was more full of the divine than Nietzsche, the stout rejector of God's existence, who coined the phrase, "The human being is something which should be transcended."

Neither should we look upon deities as chimeras of an early stage of human development, nor as mere abstractions of all those forces which are active either in nature or in our own subconsciousness: Force as such does not mean much, regardless of whether we call it life energy, vital energy, cosmic energy, or something like that. Only a formed and directed energy has the ability to be effective: It is form and direction which let a power become reality. For example, the power of rays of light is close to zero. But if the same rays pass through a piece of magnifing glass, they can induce flames.

Of all formed and forming forces it is only our consciousness—whose visible expression is our own body—which is immediately accessible to us. If, through meditative effort, we have learned to stay totally in the present, we will realize that each act of awareness has a formative power. It contributes to the creation and change of our own individual shape by forming anew in each moment our unity of mind and body *(nama-rupa)*, i.e., it is equally effective on the level of both matter and spirit. But this is not all of its effects. Like a magnetic field, its results are not limited to the point of origin: They also affect the environment in all directions, and they influence—depending on the strength of the original impulse—other centers of consciousness and further, the whole of personality.

The intensity of the effect, however, is not dependent so much on the amount of the original energy itself as on the clarity and plasticity of the creative imagination. The ideas of Christianity would never have affected the world to such a degree if Christ's sacrificial death on the cross had not been such a pictorial symbol. The Buddha, too, would never have been able to be influential beyond his time and the limits of the Indian subcontinent if he had not succeeded in explaining the truths he found in a plastic and evocative form. (Let's just think of the convincing power of Prince Siddhartha's four encounters during his four outings. Anticipating the problem of suffering and its solution, they are appealing even today to all human beings.)

Images and visions prove to be (in the sense of the Greek word "eidos") inner experiences made visible and embodied as formative forces that are capable of shaking and profoundly influencing the world. These are no dry fancies, but powers that create reality. Among these images are some that are not only the spiritual property of selected individuals, mystic cults, or highly developed cultures, but are shared by the whole of mankind, which reaches in these "innate images" a climax of creativity. Although the forms these archetypes can assume are subject to change, they all originate in that elemental yearning which was mentioned above, and are capable of inducing—if arising spontaneously—a similar experience which can only be hinted at by the word "liberation." Whenever this yearning reaches its highest level of intensity, and as soon as the conditions are right or favorable, the awareness of human beings condenses into one of these innate images, which then embodies itself in the form of a god, a divine hero, or a savior.

And this deity (or the deity in the form of the divine hero, or the savior) lives and exerts his influence literally as long as there are human beings who nurture him with the powers of their innermost being through love and devotion. He grows in correspondence to the intensity with which his devotees enliven him in their minds and, conversely, to the extent that he is capable of keeping himself alive in the awareness of the people. And this is how he develops himself and remains active until finally it is time for him, too, to strive for his own salvation—to completely let go. And then? Silence—twilight of the gods—or descend to the world of human beings for a new and final transformation.

Although we are not endowed with universal or divine power, by opening to its influence, we can create within ourselves the readiness to become receptive to it. Light is always present, but as long as we shut it out, we remain in the dark. Even the highest power requires our own willingness to cooperate. If we emphasize our egocentricity, we close ourselves off from this power which otherwise would always be accessible. But if we open ourselves to its influence, we receive it to the degree to which we surrender ourselves, i.e., our ego, our self.

The amazing fact is, that precisely at the very moment in which we are filled with this power, it will not abolish or destroy our personality. It will fill us up like a vessel, so that even at the moment when this form is breaking up and our ego-consciousness is extinguished, the uniqueness of our individuality will continue to vibrate and be transformed into a unique expression of universality which cannot be duplicated.

Power as such is not creative. It becomes creative only when meeting resistance. This is why the universal is dependent on the individual, the divine within the human being, in order to recognize itself. This is *lila*, the cosmic play, of which Angelus Silesius, the German Christian mystic, said:

I know that without myself,
God could not exist for even a single moment:
If I would expire,
he would have to die in despair.

The higher the tension or the distance between both poles, the more there is creativity, or the power for insight and realization. The danger of the West is to overemphasize the pole of individuality, and therefore ego-activity and willpower. The East, however, is always tempted to overemphasize the pole of universality, and therefore to deny the value of individuality, which can lead to passive disintegration and self-dissolution in an amorphous unity.

151

Both attitudes are therefore in conflict with the inherent laws of all existence: the one, by suppressing the universal, the other, by denying the value of individuality. The latter attitude, however, completely contradicts the idea of a "divine universe," as it is taught by many Hindu schools, because this would amount to accusing the conceived divine power of having senselessly created a world of individual forms. Therefore, overemphasizing unity (as, for example, in Shankaracharya's monistic *Advaitavada*) turns out to be as big an error as that of duality or plurality.

If we consider duality as an unbridgeable antagonism or mere opposition, and not as a natural polarity of the same appearance, or if we take sides for only one part of such a unity, by negating and totally eliminating the other side, then we suffer from one of the worst of illusions. However, if we attempt to deny the fact of polarity (by maintaining that all things are in their essence basically the same), then we live in an even bigger illusion, because we are closing our eyes before the most obvious facts of experience.

Like a drunkard who has lost all sense of distinctions believes that he is living in a state of perfect brotherhood and harmony with all and everything around, since he has numbed his sense of individuality and self-responsibility—in the same way those cheat themselves who believe they have reached the highest goal, or a state of divine unification, when they are lost in an unconscious "samadhi" or trancelike state of mind. Only those who succeed in bringing their knowledge of universality into the activities of a regular human life have achieved something worthwhile. Those who are incapable of doing that may succeed in escaping their problems for a while but are prone to become as addicted to abnormal trance or self- hypnosis as to a drug.

Individuality—that which cannot be separated—is not an unchangeable, eternal "soul"; it is a continuous direction within constant change. This is because what makes us an individual is not the "eternity" of our psyche, but the awareness of continuity on our path, which we follow according to our respective level of development and the corresponding changes of our inner attitude. According to Buddhist understanding, individuality is therefore the result of constant, uncompromising, and consistent transformation in the process of spiritual growth.

All contents of our consciousness are by necessity dependent on our respective biological center. However, that by no means implies that they are limited by the ego in the sense of an overemphasized egocentricity. Although the prerequisite for each experience is a subject who has the experience, this experience does not necessarily require the belief in a continuous or eternal unchanging self. For example, the ego of a person who is looking at a particularly beautiful sunset, or is listening to a marvelous symphony, is totally irrelevant. After the memory of such an experience sinks into our subconscious, there remains nothing of our ego.

The transformation of our dark, unconscious impulses and reactions into light and clear thoughts and contemplations, which lead to spontaneous visualizations within meditation, are—as C. G. Jung once remarked—in the true sense of the word a "second cosmic creation."

Already on early levels of biological and physiological processes we can recognize a meaningfully and consequently working force which is creating and sustaining an organism capable of repeatedly regenerating itself by selecting and assimilating organic and/or inorganic substances and transforming them into a living substance which is compatible with the body. If this basis is existent, consciousness is ready for the second step on its development: It is now capable of becoming aware of itself. This gives us the first chance to liberate ourselves from the fetters of karmic entanglement.

If we worship deities, they become alive even if they never existed before, and they die when they are no longer worshipped, even if they have been in existence for millenia. This is because evocation and worship is that mental act of creation, by concentrating our consciousness on an idea, an image, a symbol, or an emotion, which is increasingly effective the more the above-mentioned components are combined. If, however, evocation and worship degenerate to mechanically and automatically performed actions or to merely intellectual and abstract concepts, they are completely ineffective.

A ritual is a technique by which an idea, image, symbol, and sensation are melted together to form a unity. As soon as rituals decline and are no longer performed, the deities die. This is the reason why, since ancient times, the exact knowledge of a ritual was considered to be the key which opens the door to those forces which manifest themselves in the deities. In order to avoid misuse, certain rituals were kept secret, especially those details considered particularly important, their correct execution being essential to the specific effectiveness of the ritual.

Genuine rituals cannot be invented or created. They grow out of the spontaneous experience of highly developed individuals in whom the accumulated religious experience and practice of many generations has become manifest. They generally crystallize around the very simple essence of a symbol or a similar symbolic action which was originally the spontaneous answer to a deeply felt emotion or insight. If these rituals are still capable of evoking a mental image in each of us, they remain powerful formative forces, since they affect both the conscious and the unconscious faculties dormant in human beings, by activating them.

155

The effect of such a ritual is twofold: individual and collective, or subjective and objective. Here we are entering the realm of "reality," thereby posing the question whether deities have an existence or not. The answer to this question cannot be gained either by logical evidence or by a speculative enumeration of all those probabilities which support it. The reality of a thing or of a force can only be demonstrated by its *effect*. However, a ritual as well as a mental image or symbol which is capable of exerting immediate effectiveness—which has taken hold of millions of human consciousnesses and has formed these people according to the inner direction of the ritual, and has also determined the actions of millions of individuals, thereby creating a super-individual field of consciousness—has to be accepted as being "objective," since it is independent of our subjective experiences and individual opinions.

Those forces, manifest in their effect, which I have simply called "deities," contain all "divine" forces and energies, regardless of whether they manifest as originally "primitive," highly developed polytheistic or pantheistic ideas, or as the realization of highest human insight and perfection, like the ones we perceive in saints, Bodhisattvas, and Buddhas in whom the human and the universal are combined in the realm of mind, in the realm of cosmic consciousness.

Therefore Buddha and the Buddhists of all times have always acknowledged the existence of deities, but without thereby deviating in the least from the essential Buddhist tenets. Only "modern" Buddhists, being under the influence of the ideas of the last century's materialistic science (a position which contemporary science has already abandoned), have a hard time accommodating to the fact that Buddha discoursed with the deities; they want to transform Buddhism into an unreligious scientific theorem.

When Buddhism became increasingly known in the last century, it was at a time intoxicated by major scientific discoveries, when the ideas of many scholars were under the sway of positivism and scientific materialism. People were looking for a "substitute" religion and thought to have discovered it in the form of an ethical and philosophical Buddhism. They neglected Buddha's words, to be found everywhere in the Pali canon, which go beyond and transcend the realm of the intellect and rationality. And in many places, up to the present day when a young generation has rediscovered the religious aspects of the Dharma, Buddhism still suffers from that heritage.

Until that time, however, Buddhism in the West was squeezed in between the fear of being considered devotional and the ambition to be "scientific." Therefore it was thought necessary to reject from the start everything accepted by Christianity, and, on the other hand, to declare everything as "Buddhistic" which could be proved by science. Without doubt, the Buddhist Dharma does not contradict any kind of scientific insights, and never will, since it regards the world according to reality and knows about the change of insight and understanding. But this does not mean that it denies a spiritual reality, which is "inaccessible to the realm of logical and discursive thinking," as Buddha declared repeatedly (for example, to Ananda when the latter understood the Pratityasamutpada as a causal chain of becoming).

Only a few groups of early European Buddhists developed a religious life which was truly alive. Most of them lacked a deeply felt ritual expression, which is only possible in the devotion to the ideal of a Buddha. In traditional Buddhist countries—regardless of whether they belong to the Theravada or the Mahayana—venerating Buddha plays an essential role. The first thing each Buddhist has to learn—whether monk or layman—are the so-called *vandana*, the formulas of veneration, which are chanted during the puja. Each puja ritual also always contains the offering of incense, light, water, and food, and culminates in three prostrations with the forehead touching the ground. This ritual is done in all temples and before all domestic altars; in the morning the offering is predominately flowers, at noon the offering of food takes a central position (especially in monasteries), and in the evening light and incense are usually offered.

One has only to visit a country in which the deities are still alive—like those regions of India which are as yet uncorrupted by Western influence, or that Tibet which I learned to know even in these times, where deities, saints, Bodhisattvas, and Buddhas were still felt as a living presence—in order to experience there the presence of those forces which modern intellectualism regards as a mere imaginary fiction or as the outcome of a mass suggestion, or as "induced mass madness."

If I am talking here of "deities," instead of using the term "god," this is not because I underestimate the value of this word, but because the concept "god" is only in a very limited way accessible to direct human experience and is therefore easily subject to intellectual speculations and wild emotions. The chilly abstraction of the monotheistic understanding of the concept "god," which Jesus tried to make more alive by the idea of the benevolent "father in heaven," may also be the reason why Christians prefer to address themselves to Jesus, Mary, and the saints, than directly to God, and that Moslems, just because of the abstract nature of Allah, which is bare of any kind of vividness, have to find a connection to God, next to the very popular veneration of saints, by a corporal ritual of deep significance and great spiritual value.

In the Roman Catholic church, this place is taken by the daily Holy Communion, the most important ritual of the Christian faith and the greatest source of power of the Catholic church. Watering down this ritual, as happened in some Protestant schools, resulted in a trend to increasingly secularize Christianity. It is therefore no wonder that in many Protestant countries the deities are dead, whereas—in the form of the saints and the Mother of God—they are still alive in the Catholic countries, mainly the southern ones, where this tradition can be traced back to the earliest times of mankind (as in the cults of mother goddesses, genii loci, lares, deceased souls, and in rituals of blessing, exorcism, protection, etc.).

The Meaning of Mantras in the Vajrayana

We have already talked about the different forms of mandalas. It is important to keep in mind that a mandala is always something which we have to visualize, to *see*. Therefore one can talk about a mandala only in as much as "seeingly" and "understandingly" one can totally absorb it. Thereby one has to know that it is always connected with a sound. And such a sound is called a mantra.

There is great confusion, however, about what is understood by mantra. Mantra means "instrument of the mind." And it *is* an instrument of the mind. Yet most people working with a mantra use neither mind nor thinking: They just repeat syllables and words which are unintelligible to them. They do not have any understanding of what the mantra they are reciting means; they babble blindly, waiting for something to happen.

But a mantra is not a magical formula. It has an inherent meaning and significance, although its meaning cannot always be expressed in words. Mantra reveals connections which go far beyond any possible literal explanation of the words. It can be compared with music, which also has an "significance" and meaningfulness which cannot be expressed in words. While words can accompany the music, they do not make the melody. In the same way as music has an inner significance and an inner meaning which cannot be expressed in words, so also mantra has a deep inner significance and an unfathomable meaning on different levels which we all have to take into account and to understand.

When discussing mantras, we have to distinguish between *bija* mantras, pure mantras, mixed mantras, and dharanis. Each of these forms refers to completely different things. The nature of a *bija* mantra antecedes language. It may be an archetypal sound which does not obey any rule of how to form words or grammatical structures. For example, let's take the *bijas* OM AH HUM HRIH TRAM. Obviously, all of these sounds do not have a real meaning. Nobody can tell what a sound like OM or HUM "means." But nevertheless we can connect it to certain meanings. In other words, each of the so-called seed mantras, or *bija* mantras, is an expression of a certain direction of movement. If, for example, we chant OM and sense something all-embracing, universal, round, like our arms moving in a circle, then we get a sense of the direction of movement this sound has.

However, it is very easy to get confused by the fact that the sound OM is used differently in Buddhism and Hinduism. In Hinduism, for example, this ancient and very beautiful sound was used in a somewhat vague way: at the beginning of a sentence or mantra, at its end, or at any other location within a sentence. But in Buddhism, it has a clearly defined place: OM can be used only at the beginning, and HUM only at the end of a combined mantra. OM always precedes a combined mantra, and HUM closes it. The reason is that OM and HUM have two different directions of movement. The OM stands for the all-inclusive universal level, whereas HUM leads into the depth of our own heart or, to put it differently, moves from the universal level down to the level of the individual. This is because we can experience the universal only as an individual. Individuality is therefore as important as universality.

In their oppositional stance OM and HUM can be compared to counterpoint in music: the one all-embracing above, and the other in the depths where our experience as human beings takes place. Buddha always pointed out very clearly that all transcendental experiences are completely useless unless we find a way to "ground" them, i.e., to put them into practice. Therefore, if we want to realize the universal within ourselves, which manifests as OM in our highest center, we first have to experience it in the depth of our heart. This is because our heart is the place where we have to look for our deepest experiences.

163

Between the OM and the HUM, which, in a way, symbolically form a vertical line, there is a movement of sound which is very different and which—in order to remain within the metaphor—forms a horizontal movement, and this is the AH. In OM AH HUM the AH expresses primarily the qualities of language: thinking, ideas, and concepts—in short, all the human qualities which are necessary for creating a culture.

Therefore the AH is assigned to the center of language, the throat center, and this is the reason why it is so important in OM AH HUM, because without language, without thinking, without ideas and concepts, without words and terms, we could not express what we are experiencing. We would be deaf and speechless, we would be a nothing. And in the same way as the OM stands for the universal level, and the HUM for the level of the human being—the level of experience within the human heart—AH stands for the level of "culture" which makes a higher consciousness possible.

There are many more *bija* mantras, such as those which are assigned to the various chakras. In this system of relations, the mantra for the throat center is the *bija* HRIH, which otherwise is related to Amitabha, the Buddha of Infinite Light, whose time is that of the setting sun. Thus, the mantra HRIH points to that area of infinite light which stands for the light of fully developed consciousness within the human mind. Although other living beings, too, have some measure of consciousness, the main difference between their consciousness and that of human beings is that they do not have a real "self"-consciousness, since, unlike humans, they cannot become aware of their own awareness. This is a specific quality and privilege of human beings, although many develop it only a little. This is why the Buddha declared that being human, or being born in the human realm, is the best of all possible rebirths, because as a human being we can become aware of our own actions and therefore can learn to act in a responsible manner. Only as a human being can we take charge of our own destiny.

However, this explanation does not exhaust the meaning of the *bija* HRIH. It is especially important that the sound HRIH has an ascending tendency, namely from the level of speech up to the thousand-petaled lotus flower, the *sahasrara* chakra, and therefore to the OM. This ascending movement is a movement toward the light, with the sound R in the HRIH pointing to the element fire, inherent in HRIH, whose *bija* is RAM.

It may not be a coincidence that in ancient Egypt, too, the sun's radiant fire was called RA, and this same RA we can also find in the *bija* TRAM, the seed syllable of the Dhyani-Buddha Ratnasambhava, whose southern position in the mandala is the time of high noon with its heat of the sun. As with all *bijas*, in the Indian Devanagari script this TRAM also ends with the *anu-svara*, a dot which indicates the mantric character of a syllable. Immediately before the RA there is a T which indicates resistance.

Thus all parts of a *bija* have a meaning, and in their complexity they point into a certain direction. And in order to make this complexity even more complex, in Buddhism each *bija* is associated not only with a certain sound, but also with a certain color and form. Those who cannot in their meditative practice wholistically understand sound, color, and form cannot grasp and "understand" the mantra.

Many people are of the opinion that the use of mantras is merely a matter of faith. Using mantras certainly requires a certain measure of confidence. But how can we develop this confidence? Confidence does not arise out of the blue. Confidence requires that we know thoroughly that in which we are supposed to have confidence. For example, if one has confidence in a certain person, then this is because one knows him, or at least one believes one knows him. In the same way, we have to know the meaning of a certain mantric sound, in which direction it is pointing, and what it stands for, before we can have confidence in a specific mantra.

Buddhism developed a very clearly defined system of mantric sounds and forms. In the monasteries and their libraries there are special books which contain more or less all mantras, simultaneously explaining their relation to certain figures of tantric visualizations.

This means, however, that at the very moment in which we are chanting a certain mantra, with our inner eye we have to visualize the figure, color, movement, and gesture which all together form a total unity. With this we gain an understanding of what I call "the background" for spiritual working with mantras. For those who do not know the religious background of a certain mantra, that mantra is without meaning and therefore without transformative power: It is merely an empty sound. Therefore I dare to say that a person who teaches mantras without explaining their background, without giving an introduction, without giving a real initiation into a particular mantra, is doing something completely senseless.

Now there are mantras which contain other mantric words besides the *bijas*, which are located between OM and HUM (or between OM and SVAHA). For example, the famous mantra OM MANI PADME HUM is such a "combined" mantra. While OM and HUM are *bijas*, i.e., seed mantras, the two words in between can be translated, because the words MANI and PADMA have a meaning, or better, various meanings on different levels. Literally translated, MANI PADME means "jewel in the lotus flower." But who or what is the jewel? On the one hand, the jewel is Buddha, Dharma, and Sangha; here we connect the word "jewel" with a meaning which transcends the meaning associated with a precious stone. On the other hand, the precious jewel is also the Buddha as embodiment of realized enlightenment,

167

which is the potentiality of our innermost being. PADMA stands for our spiritual center, our "heart." Grammatically, PADME is a locative, meaning "within the lotus flower," i.e., within the heart—not our physical heart, but our innermost spiritual center.

Often there are attempts to translate this mantra in various ways, mostly with little ingenuity. For example, OM is translated as "Oh!" and HUM as "amen." The middle part is rendered as "jewel in the lotus flower" or "dew drop in the lotus flower." However, translations like these are useless and warp the meaning of the mantra. Unfortunately, scholars all over the world have until now shown little interest in mantras, some of them even declaring that mantras are "meaningless babblings" which do not deserve serious consideration. Thus Indologists and scholars of theology doing research in Hinduism and Buddhism skipped over mantras as if they were without meaning.

If one learns a little more about life in Tibet, one sees how deeply rooted mantras are in the minds of the people. Many chant their mantra even while walking, working, or traveling. With each step they take, they repeat their mantra in a rhythmical fashion in order to maintain that specific sensation which connects them to their religious practice or their specific visualization. The mantra is repeated in order to create uninterrupted mindfulness of the inner vision, or to recall it anew into consciousness at any time. Since the practitioner connects the mantra directly with the various forms of the Buddhas and the wisdoms associated with them, chanting the mantra strengthens mindfulness and mental clarity. At that moment, however, when repetition of the mantra turns into a mechanical process, the mantra becomes meaningless, an empty sound.

In Tibet, a *mani-khorlo,* erroneously translated as "prayer mill," is often used as a means for concentration.[1] It is turned in the direction of the movement of the sun, i.e., in a clockwise direction. It has constantly to be kept in motion; at the moment when attention is directed to something else, the movement will stop. Therefore it is evident that using a *mani-khorlo* is nothing mechanical: It is accompanied by a movement of our mind and is therefore symbolically reminiscent of Buddha's first sermon in the Deer Park, the *Dharma-chakra-pravartana,* the "Setting in Motion the Wheel of the Dharma."

But what is this Dharma? For Buddha, the Dharma was more than merely a moral religious law. Although it also contains suggestions for moral and ethical conduct according to the individual's insight, Buddha understood the Dharma as universal law. On the level of human beings, universal law leads to ethics, so long as we keep in mind that each of us has to set the Dharmachakra in motion within himself, in the same way as Buddha did, too. Only then will we move in the direction which he indicated as the path of liberation.

169

In Buddhism, it is not sufficient to think that Buddha set the wheel of the Dharma in motion for us, and all we have to do is to chant and repeat his words. If the wheel of the Dharma does not stay in motion within ourselves, then what Buddha did twenty-five hundred years ago was of no avail.

But now let's have a look at a mixed mantra. We know various mixed mantras, some of which refer to certain aspects of Buddhahood or to specific functions such as energy, compassion, or discriminative wisdom; for each of these aspects there is a specific mantra. This already makes it obvious that one should not chant mantras without knowledge of their background. If mantras were dependent only on faith, then just *one* mantra would be sufficient to satisfy all our needs for our whole life. It would be unnecessary to have different mantras. But this we often forget. Therefore I want to repeat: If one knows neither the direction of a mantra, nor the visualization that goes with it, then one should not use the mantra.

Now let's go on to the dharanis. What actually is a dharani? They are often confused with mantras and many believe that they are the same. Dharanis, however, are formulas which attempt to allow for a concentration or fixation of the mind. To put it differently: One uses a dharani in order to direct the mind to something and to increasingly concentrate it in this way. For example, let's take one of the most famous dharanis, which is known as the "Hundred Syllables

170

Mantra." This hundred syllables mantra, originally directed to Vajrasattva, was soon also directed to Avalokiteshvara and other Mahasattvas.

The example of this dharani makes it evident in which way it differs from a pure mantra: It can be translated word by word. But if one does not know the translation, merely speaking it is meaningless. And this is where questions arise. In China, for example, where Sanskrit was not known, some of these Sanskrit formulas were taught more than a thousand years ago. But eventually the mantras or dharanis became warped because the people could neither speak the words properly nor did they know their meaning. Therefore these mantras and dharanis degenerated to a kind of magical formula which in the course of time lost all meaning. Today nobody in China understands them; they are just meaningless syllables. Although people have great faith in these formulas, they do not know their meaning.

In the following, I will take the example of the Hundred Syllables Mantra and demonstrate how such a formula can be translated from the Sanskrit. This dharani, in particular, plays an important role in Tibet, although even there it is chanted by many people without understanding of its real meaning. Originally the Sanskrit mantras were pronounced properly in Tibet, and for those who know the system of transliteration from Devanagari into the Tibetan alphabet, even today the original Sanskrit form can be reconstructed. Even if now the pronunciation differs from the original, the proper meaning and form can still be recognized. For example, if the Tibetans say PEME instead of PADMA, and SATTO instead of SATTVA, it does not matter much, because they know what the words PEME and SATTO stand for and what they mean in their Sanskrit form.

All this contradicts those who believe that a mantra is effective only because of its sound vibrations. From a philological point of view, the Tibetans and the other East Asian peoples have been mispronouncing the Sanskrit words for millenia, out of ignorance sometimes even splitting up Sanskrit word groups. But nevertheless the mantras remained as effective there as if they were still pronounced in the proper manner. This proves that a mantra consists not merely of sound vibrations and is effective not merely because of its sound oscillations. What counts are the vibrations of our mind. Our mind is the mediator between the mantra and its result: We have to create the energy of a mantra within ourselves in order to release it effectively. If there is no movement within ourselves, the mantra is ineffective, and this is the reason why many people who chant mantras never experience their transformative power.

On the other hand, there are always people who think that with the help of a mantra they can magically bypass the laws of nature. However, no mantra will ever violate nature. The effect of a mantra is always in harmony with the laws of nature. It is only that these laws are much more encompassing than we usually believe. A mantra can intensify certain natural laws, but this does not mean they are no longer valid.

But let's now go on to Vajrasattva's Hundred Syllables Mantra:

OM VAJRASATTVA SAMAYAM — ANUPALAYA
VAJRASATTVA TVEN OPATISHTHA : DRITTHO ME BHAVA
SUTOSHYO ME BHAVA
SUPOSHYO ME BHAVA
ANURAKTO ME BHAVA
SARVA SIDDHIM ME PRAYACCHA
SARVA KARMASU CA
ME CITTAM SHREYAH KURU HUM
HAHA HAHA HOH
BHAGAVAN SARVA TATHAGATA VAJRA
MA ME MUNCA
VAJRI BHAVA MAHASAMAYA — SATTVA AH!

The translation is as follows:

OM Vajrasattva, protector of the vow!
Vajrasattva, with your support let
me become steadfast!
Let me become (be) content,
grant me all siddhas,
and in all (my) deeds
let my mind be more competent, HUM!
Haha haha hoh!

173

Most exalted diamond of all Tathagatas:
do not forsake me.
May the diamond, the embodiment of
the Great Vow (be realized)! AH!

As we can see, a meaningful translation word by word of the whole dharani is possible, whereby the content can be meditated upon in any language. But if one knows the meaning of the words, one can also use the Sanskrit text to let the words stand out from the ordinary way of speaking.

This dharani, which characterizes the beginning of the path and is helpful when taking the first steps on the way, inspired many people for millenia. However, it can inspire only if through meditation we come to an understanding of its meaning, which then guides our actions. Without initiation into the meaning and significance of the dharani, without the thereby gained understanding of the direction this mantra has and the accompanying visualization of Vajrasattva, this dharani, too, remains lifeless.

Nowadays people often take a book which contains mantras and, without real understanding, start chanting them. The effect equals zero. It is a meaningless action, because the sounds chanted are without life. This is because a mantra is filled with life only when given by a guru in an initiation, i.e., by somebody who is our personal spiritual teacher and who first explains the significance of this mantra: the background against which it stands and with which it is closely connected, such as colors, visualizations, mudras, etc. Only when this basis has been established can the mantra be transmitted as the closing act of an initiation.

Thus one can have a real initiation only after having sufficiently studied the basic facts. The mantra, given during initiation, becomes the adept's lifelong "root mantra." Throughout his life it connects him with the one who gave the initiation. Whenever this mantra is chanted, one will see one's guru with the mind's eye and feel being in his presence, sensing always anew that great inspiration which the guru installed in a rudimentary form when he let his student participate in his own realization. And thus the practitioner is always reminded newly of the direction in which he has to go: He knows his goal, he knows the taste of realization; he is not a blind adherent.

Previously I mentioned Guru Padmasambhava's mantra OM AH HUM VAJRA GURU PADMA SIDDHI HUM. It is possible to clearly define this mantra. There are in Devanagari—as well as in the Tibetan alphabet—the three word-symbol units for OM AH HUM, the *bija* mantras which represent the universal level, the level of culture or ideals, and that of human beings. Only if these three levels have been recognized and realized can one penetrate to an understanding of the Vajra Guru. The word "Vajra Guru" has a special significance. It is the primeval guru, brilliantly radiating, of diamond-like hardness, transparent and pure like a

diamond. The PADMA SIDDHI HUM points to that which
one has to fulfill and bring to completion. SIDDHI means
completion, mastery, while PADMA points to the heart
chakra in our own inner center, the location where the
great transformation takes place. Thus, knowing the
meaning of the different mantric words, we can now
proceed to increasingly experience them in our meditation, wholistically, in their total connectedness.

The same mantric preparatory work has to be done
when we are using a mandala. In the previous lectures
we mentioned that the four directions have four different colors, which surround the center, which also
has a color. Furthermore, to each direction a mantra is
assigned. For example, in the mandala of the Dhyani
Buddhas, the four directions are characterized in a
clockwise fashion from east to north by the *bijas* HUM
TRAM HRIH AH, and the center by the *bija* OM. If the
mantras are chanted in connection with a mandala,
one knows what one has to visualize. With HUM,
Akshobhya is to be visualized, located in the east; with
TRAM, Ratnasambhava in the south, etc. In the center
of the mandala resides Vairochana, who embodies the
wisdom of all Buddhas and is therefore represented
by the universal sound OM.

The different Buddhas of the directions stand for
various aspects of our consciousness. Thus, Buddha
Akshobhya, located in the east, where the sun is rising, is the manifestation of the first step of our still
reflective thinking. He is characterized by a mirror and

a vajra and radiates white light, emitted by a blue figure. But what does that mean?

If we are entering the mandala, we first have to regard the world like an image in a mirror. In it we recognize the nature of the world as it is: past, present, and future in a continuous process of becoming and changing. We also recognize our own participation in the stream of becoming of this world in which we all are living. Only if we have dared to regard the world as it is in reality can we think and feel with other living beings. Thus, the eastern position, in which our mental attitude is characterized by the earth-touching gesture *(bhumisparsha-mudra)*, makes us aware that our roots are deeply connected with the earth, and that we have to learn that the earth is our own past.

At that moment in which we "seeingly" recognize ourselves and the world in which we are living, we can think of other living beings. But then the hand-mirror in which we gaze at ourselves turns by itself and points outward: We now turn totally toward others. Although we are still aware of ourselves, we are no longer ego-centered; we are no longer concerned merely with ourselves. If one turns the palm outward, then this is a gesture of giving and indicates that one is in communication with the world, or better: that we are giving ourselves to the world. This is the meaning of the *dana-mudra,* the gesture of giving.

When we give ourselves totally to communication with other living beings, we recognize the essential sameness of all beings, but at the same time we learn to understand and to appreciate their differences. It is not our intention to do away with differences, but to recognize the divine inherent in each individual which manifests as his specific traits and manners of expressing himself. In acknowledging diversity, we no longer attempt to make others be the same way we are, but realize the greatness of life in the richness of its various forms of manifestation. This is expressed in the gesture of meditation, Amitabha's *dhyana-mudra*.

Amoghasiddhi, the Buddha of the northern position, is characterized by the gesture of fearlessness, the *abhaya-mudra*. Here the gesture of prayer is raised to the level of the heart. This means that we have now reached a higher level in which we are raised above the world and are blessing it while at the same time we are active within it, all feelings of fear having fallen away. However, fear can only be overcome by compassion: From now on our actions will be based on compassion, no longer on egocentric concerns. Only this kind of action is free of karma, and therefore this gesture expresses the wisdom by which all actions are fulfilled.

In this way, we slowly approach the center from which the pure light of Buddhahood radiates, the light of *dharmakaya*. To put it differently: Buddhahood can only be found in the realization of all those qualities which, taken all together, form the richness of the mandala. This central wisdom, embodied in Vairochana, cannot immediately be experienced. We have to approach it step by step, initially learning to distinguish between different qualities, until finally we are able to experience wholeness in the unity of opposites. This is why we circumambulate the center in a clockwise direction: Without full experience of the periphery, the center cannot be understood. Therefore we circulate around the center again and again, in a spiraling fashion approaching the center, until we can totally merge with it.

This is what I call the symphonic movement of meditation. And meditation is really a kind of symphony in which four motifs are played again and again in different variations. The first leitmotif is the wisdom of the great mirror, the second the wisdom of the essential unity of all living beings. The third is the discriminating, visionary wisdom of meditation, which indicates that meditation is not just a mental state in which we indiscriminately dissolve into each and everything, but that here we arrive at an understanding of the always present differences and discontinue projecting our own ideas on other forms of existence. We realize that each being is a distinct and unique expression of the whole. After we have passed through the discriminative wisdom, we finally arrive at the wisdom which completes all actions: the inner attitude of compassion. After having completely developed compassion for all sentient beings and for the whole world, we finally approach the wisdom of *dharmadhatu*, and thereby the completion of our path to Buddhahood for the sake of all living beings.

Notes

1. Lama Govinda here refers to the German word "Gebetsmuehle," which literally means "prayer mill" and has a negative, mechanical connotation. *Mani-khorlo* is usually translated into English as "prayer wheel."

TERMINOLOGY
& INDEX

Significant Terms

Term*	Sanskrit	Pāli
abhaya	abhaya	abhaya-mudra
advaitavada	advaitavāda	
ahimsa	ahimsa	ahimsa
Akshobhya	Akṣobhya	
Amitabha	Amitābha	
Amoghasiddhi	Amoghasiddhi	
amrita-kalasha	amṛta-kalaśa	amata-kalasa
Ananda	Ānanda	Ānanda
anatman	anatman	anattā
anusvara	anusvāra	
Arhat	Arhat	Arahant
artha	artha	attha
ashtangikamarga	aṣṭāṅgikamārga	aṭṭhāṅgika-magga
atman	atman	attā
Avalokiteshvara	Avalokiteśvara	
avidya	avidyā	avijjā
Bhasadhara	Bhāsadharā	
bhava	bhava	bhava
bhavanga-sota	bhavāṅga-srota	bhavāṅga-sota
bhikshu	bhikṣu	bhikkhu
bhumisparsha	bhūmisparśa	
bija	bīja	bīja

*As it appears in the text

Significant Terms

Term	Sanskrit	Pāli
Bodhisattva	Bodhisattva	Bodhisatta
Buddhaghosha	Buddhaghoṣa	Buddhaghosa
chakra	cakra	cakka
ceto-vimutti	citta-vimukti	ceto-vimutti
chetana	cetanā	cetanā
damaru	ḍamaru	
dana	dāna	
devadevanam	devādevānām	
dharani	dhāraṇī	
dharma	dharma	Dhamma
Dharmachakra	Dharmacakra	Dhammacakka
Dharmadhatu	Dharmadhātu	Dhammadhātu
Dharmakaya	Dharmakāya	Dhammakāya
dhyana	dhyāna	jhāna
dhyani	dhyāni	
guru	guru	
ida	iḍā	
Isipathana	Ṛsipathana	Isipathana
Jataka	Jātaka	Jātaka
jara-marana	jarā-maraṇa	jarā-maraṇa
jati	jāti	jāti
kalpa	kalpa	kappa
Kanishka	Kaniṣka	
kapala	kapāla	
karuna	karuṇā	karuṇā
karma	karma	kamma
khatvanga	khaṭvāṅga	
krodha-bhairava	krodha-bhairava	
Lankavatara	Laṅkāvatāra	
lila	līlā	
Mahakala	Mahākāla	
Mahayana	Mahāyāna	
maitri	maitrī	metta
mandala	maṇḍala	
Mandarava	Mandāravā	

183

Significant Terms

Term	Sanskrit	Pāli
mani	mani	mani
mantra	mantra	
mitra	mitra	mitta
mudita	muditā	muditā
mudra	mudrā	
nama-rupa	nāma-rūpa	nāma-rūpa
Nirmanakaya	Nirmāṇakāya	
nirvana	nirvāṇa	nibbāna
padma	padma	
Padmasambhava	Padmasambhava	
pandit	paṇḍita	
Parinirvana	Parinirvāṇa	Parinibbāna
pingala	piṅgala	
prajna	prajñā	paññā
Prajnaparamita	Prajñāpāramitā	
prana	prāṇa	pāṇa
pratityasamutpada	pratīyasamutpāda	paṭiccasamuppāda
Pratyekabuddha	Pratyekabuddha	Paccekabuddha
puja	pūjā	
Rahula	Rāhula	Rāhula
sadayatana	saḍāyatāna	salāyatana
sadhu	sādhu	sādhu
sahasrara	sahasrāra	
Sambhogakaya	Sambhogakāya	
samyak-drishti	samyak-dṛṣṭi	sammā-diṭṭi
-samadhi	-samādhi	-samādhi
-samkalpa	-samkalpa	-samkappa
-sambuddha	-sambuddha	-sambuddha
samskara	samskāra	saṅkhāra
sanatana	sanātana	
samkhya	samkhya	
Sanskrit	Sanskrt	
Sarasvati	Sarasvātī	
Savari	Śavari	
shabda	śabda	sadda

Significant Terms

Term	Sanskrit	Pāli
Shakyamuni	Śākyamuni	
shila	śīla	sīla
shramana	śramaṇa	samaṇa
shunyata	śūnyatā	suññatā
siddha	siddha	
Siddhartha	Siddhārtha	
siddhi	siddhi	iddhi
sparsha	sparśa	
sushumna	suṣumnā	
Sutra	Sūtra	Sutta
Tantra	Tantra	
Tathagata	Tathāgata	Tathāgata
Theravadin	Theravādin	Theravādin
trishna	tṛṣṇā	taṇhā
trishula	triśula	
upadana	upādāna	upādāna
upaya	upāya	upāya
upeksha	upekṣā	upekkhā
vahan	vāhana	
Vairochana	Vairocana	
Vaisakha	Vaiśākha	Visākha
vajra	vajra	
Vajradhara	Vajradhara	
Vajrapani	Vajrapāṇi	
Vajrasattva	Vajrasattva	
Vajrayana	Vajrayāna	
vandana	vandana	
varna	varṇa	vaṇṇa
vedana	vedanā	vedanā
vijnana	vijñāna	viññāṇa
vimukta	vimukta	vimutta
virya	vīrya	viriya
vishvavajra	viśvavajra	
yajna	yajña	
yatha-bhutam	yathā-bhūtam	yathā-bhūta

Dharma Classifications

SANSKRIT	TIBETAN	ENGLISH
triratna	dkon-mchog-gsum	three jewels
Buddha	sangs-rgyas	The Enlightened One
Dharma	chos	The Teaching
Samgha	dge-'dun	The Enlightened Assembly
triyāna	thegs-pa-gsum	three vehicles
śrāvakayāna	nyan-thos-kyi-theg-pa	vehicle of listeners
pratyeka-buddhayāna	rang-sangs-rgyas-kyi-theg-pa	vehicle of the solitary realizers
bodhisattvayāna	byang-chub-sems-dpa'i-theg-pa	vehicle of the altruistic saints
caturāryasatya	'phags-pa'i-bden-pa-bzhi	four noble truths
duḥkha	sdug-bsngal	suffering
samudaya	kun-'byung-ba	source of suffering
nirodha	'gog-pa	cessation of suffering
mārga	lam	path leading to the cessation of suffering
apramāṇa	tshad-med-pa-bzhi	four immeasuables
maitrī	byams-pa	love
karuṇā	thugs-rje	compassion
muditā	dga'-ba	joy
upekṣā	btang-snyoms	equanimity

aṣṭāṅga-āryamārga	'phags-pa'i-lam-yan-lag-brgyad-pa	eightfold noble path
samyag-dṛṣṭi	yang-dag-pa'i-lta-ba	right view
samyak-samkalpa	yang-dag-pa'i-rtog-pa	right intention
samyag-vāk	yang-dag-pa'i-ngag	right speech
samyak-karmānta	yang-dag-pa'i-las-kyi-mtha'	right conduct
samyak-ājīva	yang-dag-pa'i-'tsho-ba	right livelihood
samyag-vyāyāma	yang-dag-pa'i-rtsol-ba	right effort
samyak-smṛti	yang-dag-pa'i-dran-pa	right mindfulness
samyak-samādhi	yang-dag-pa'i-ting-nge-'dzin	right concentration

pratityasamutpāda nidāna	rten-'brel-yan-lag-bcu-gnyis	twelve links of dependent origination
avidyā	ma-rig-pa	ignorance
samskāra	'du-byed	karmic dispositions
vijñāna	rnam-par-shes-pa	consciousness
nāmarūpa	ming-dang-gzugs	name and form
ṣaḍāyatanāni	skye-mched-drug	six senses
sparśa	reg-pa	contact
vedanā	tshor-ba	feeling
tṛṣṇā	sred-pa	craving
upādāna	nye-bar-len-pa	grasping
bhava	srid-pa	existence
jāti	skye-ba	birth
jarāmaraṇa	rga-shi	old age and death

Index

and sound, 165–166
birth *(jati)*, 98
Bodhisattva, 39, 40, 120, 156, 159
  ideal, 40, 65
  path, 78
body, 96
  as expression of universe, 96
Brahma, 20, 33, 66
Brahman, 39
Brahmanas, 31,
Brahmanic tradition, 32
Brahmanism, 13, 14, 15, 19, 23, 34, 92
  pre-Brahmanism, 94
brahmin, 16, 17, 18
breath, 130–33, 135
Buddha (Shakyamuni Buddha), 15, 20ff, 38ff, 42, 43, 44, 59ff, 65ff, 119, 122–23, 130, 132, 134, 137ff, 165ff
  activities of, 59–60
  artistic representation of, 69
  as "Great Shramana," 93
  depictions of, 139–40
  four main events, 80
  life as symbol, 141
  nature of, 65, 143–45
  qualities of, 59–60, 69, 70, 139, 140
  Samyaksambuddha, 67
  spiritual lineage, 142
Buddhadharma, 115
Buddhaghosha, 67

Buddhahood, 59, 61, 66, 67, 68, 82, 145, 170, 180
Buddhas, 156, 159, 169
  of past and future, 142
Buddhism, 13ff, 37ff, 44ff, 62ff,63ff, 72ff, 80ff, 93ff, 113ff, 141ff, 157ff, 163ff
  in the West, 157
  central teachings of, 95ff
  early schools, 65
  roots of, 93
  Tibetan, 8, 36ff

chakra, 116, 117
caste system, 16, 17
Catholic church, 159–60
cave temples, 9
Ch'an (school), 44, 45
change, 133, 153
chaos, 146
chela, 136
chos, 36
Christ, 39, 40, 42, 43, 149
Christians, 14, 159
Christianity, 15, 36ff, 149, 157, 160
Chuan-teng Lu, 54
circumambulation, 80
  path of *(pradakshina-patha)*, 81
code of ethics, 18
color as symbol, 82, 124, 125
compassion *(karuna)*, 93, 112, 117, 135, 178
conceptualization, 122
confidence, 115

energetic potential *(virya)*, 111
energy, 31
Enlightened Mind, 37, 144
enlightenment, 39, 68, 80, 82,
    143
    of the Buddha, 59–60, 82,
    137, 138
Eno, Patriarch, *aka* Hui-Neng,
    46, 47
error, 46
eternity, 47
ethical responsibility, 92
Evans-Wentz, 75
experience, 89ff, 114ff
    meditative, 96
    of breath *(anapanasati)*, 132
    religious, 90ff
    subjective, 89
    transcendental, 90, 96
    universal, 92
expression, linguistic, 122

fate, 20
feelings *(vedana)*, 98
five jinas. *See* Dhyani Buddhas
formative powers *(samskara)*,
    98
freedom, 131

Ganden, 38
Gandhara, 69
Gandhi, 17
Goethe, 91
God, 39, 69, 147, 151, 159
Goddard, Dwight, 101
gods, 7, 19, 23, 26, 65, 69

and goddesses, 20. *See also*
    deities
grasping *(upadana)*, 98
great death, 130
Great Perfection *(rDzogs-
    chen)*, 77
Greece, 16
greed, 100
Guge, 40, 41, 42
gurus, 115, 120

halo, 61, 62
Harappa, 22, 94
hatred, 100
hell, 62
hells, eight great, 53
Heraclitus, 108
Heruka, 79
Himalayas, 3ff
Hinayana, 67, 77
Hindu, origin of name, 93
Hinduism, 13ff, 34, 93, 94
Hindus, 22, 123
Holy Communion, 159
Hui-Neng. *See* Eno
human being, 165
    value of, 165
Hundred Syllables Mantra,
    170–71, 173–74

iconography, 63
ida, 73, 77
ignorance *(avidya)*, 97–98, 100
illusion, 28, 29, 152
images, 149
immortality, 73